Louie, Take a Look at This!

My Time with Huell Howser

Luis Fuerte
as told to David Duron

PROSPECT
·PARK·
BOOKS

Photo Credits
Cover image and pages 8, 13, 16, 48, 68, 82, 91, 92, 106, 109, 128, 150, 158, 160, 165, 166, 168, 174, and 187, courtesy of the Leatherby Libraries at Chapman University
Page 14, courtesy of Harriett Howser Weems
Page 18, courtesy of WCBS New York
Page 19, courtesy of WSMV-TV Nashville
Pages 24, 25, and 26, courtesy of Luis Fuerte
Page 28, courtesy of D. Converse
Pages 34, 36, 44, 63, 65, 84, 86, 96, 99, 100, 113, 116, 124, 130, 134, 136, 139, 141, 142, 143, and 180, courtesy of KCET
Page 60, courtesy of Craig T. Mathew/Mathew Imaging
Page 110, photograph by Ann Anderson
Page 115, courtesy of Harry Thomason

Published by Prospect Park Books
2359 Lincoln Avenue
Altadena, CA 91001
www.prospectparkbooks.com

Distributed by Consortium Book Sales & Distribution
www.cbsd.com

Library of Congress Cataloging in Publication Data is on file with the Library of Congress. The following is for reference only:
Names: Fuerte, Luis, author; Duron, David, co-author
Title: Louie, take a look at this! My time with Huell Howser
Identifiers: ISBN 9781945551024 (hardcover) | ISBN 9781945551031 (ebook)
Subjects: Huell Howser—Biography. | Huell Howser and Luis Fuerte—Memoir. | "California's Gold"—television.

Book layout and design by Amy Inouye, Future Studio

I dedicate this book to my lovely wife, Gloria,
for her support, inspiration, and encouragement,
and to all the people who have told their stories
to Huell Howser (and later, to David Duron),
for without them this book would not be possible.

"All you have to do is open your eyes and have a sense of adventure and go out and find them for yourself. I'm convinced that if you put a spotlight on any person or any subject, and you're genuinely interested in them, you can make something people enjoy watching."

— Huell Howser

CONTENTS

Introduction

THAT'S AMAAAZING!

I'm Louie. I'm the cameraman who Huell Howser called out to in KCET's beloved series *California's Gold*. Viewers so often heard him exclaim, "Louie, take a look at this!" but I rarely went in front of the camera. My given name is Luis Alejandro Fuerte, but I'm more comfortable with Luis or Louie.

This is the story of the twelve years I worked with Huell as his cameraman. It's not only the account of my personal recollections of the conversations, events, and experiences Huell and I shared during our years working together, but also the stories of the people we knew, both professionally and as guests in the shows. Most of all, it's the story of two people with personalities and backgrounds so dissimilar, one wouldn't think the two of us could ever get along. Yet our differences are what made us so perfectly matched as the shooting team you knew and loved on *California's Gold, Visiting with Huell Howser,* and many other television productions.

It is my hope that you'll enjoy reading about all of these things as our story unfolds, and that you'll find more than just interesting tidbits about Huell Howser. I also need to say that this project never could have happened without David Duron, a former producer at KCET and the man who helped me get these stories written, find photographs, and make the project happen. By the time you're done with it, I hope you'll come away pleased that you got to know the big, smiling man from Tennessee as I knew him.

As I listened to Huell on our shoots, talking to people from all walks of life throughout the state of California, I came to realize that he was genuinely and deeply interested in the people he interviewed and their personal stories. He was truly fascinated with his discoveries, from the stupendous to the downright ordinary. They all mattered to him. And he especially loved the history of California, his adopted state.

Knowing how much Huell cared about all these people, and California, inspired and even compelled me to do the best I could as his cameraman, so he could tell his stories exactly as he wanted them told. I am still saddened by the unexpected passing of my old friend and shooting partner. Every time I think of him, I can still hear his friendly Southern voice and the exuberant reactions to his discoveries—most famously, this rousing and endearing exclamation: "That's amaaazing!"

MEETING HUELL

The year was 1987. In Los Angeles, KCET-TV was in the swing of
the Golden Age of Television, and I was enjoying working there as
an engineer. The public television station's big production stages
were busy with both national and local programs, and remote units were
stationed at the Dorothy Chandler Pavilion and other Southern California theaters to cover a variety of marvelous performances. It was a time
of innovative, even daring productions that the area's dozen or so commercial television stations either couldn't or wouldn't ever consider
doing. And then came a local KCET show called *Videolog*.

The idea behind *Videolog* was for a reporter-producer to make a
three- to six-minute show about interesting people from all walks of
life in Southern California. The stories were to be aired between regular programs when they ran short. In the television industry, these are
called "interstitial programs." We just called them fillers.

To put it plainly, these little shows were major pains in the butt
for the engineers (that's what we early cameramen were, engineers)
who shot them—not because they weren't the high and mighty productions we liked to do, but because, more often than not, we had to
go on all-day shoots with producers and came back with incomplete or

half-baked stories. Often, producers would shoot everything in sight yet they'd still forget something and we'd have to go back out to shoot the missing elements—all for only a few minutes of story.

Then along came Huell Howser.

I first met Huell that year when I was assigned to shoot a *Videolog* episode for him. I saw an imposing man: about six-four and handsome, with short blond hair and big muscles showing through a tight shirt. Add an even bigger Tennessee-flavored voice, and you had a man who stood out from everyone else. I had heard that he was on the lot before that shoot—the word around the station was that he'd been hired to shoot *Videolog*s on the side while he also worked at KCBS Channel 2 doing short features that ran in its news programs. I wish I could remember what we shot on that first *Videolog* we did together, but we did so many episodes and saw so much that those early shoots are all kind of lumped together in my head.

Huell worked with many cameramen on his *Videolog* shoots, so getting to work with him was hit or miss. And we all wanted to work with him, because we saw that the man with the heavy Tennessee accent really knew his stuff. I recall that his style of shooting on *Videolog* was simple and straightforward. I'm pretty sure that Huell came to shoots with the whole story already in his head; he knew what he wanted the story to look like, how it should flow and develop, and he did his setups carefully to make sure his vision would happen.

By working with Huell on the *Videolog* shows, a good cameraman who saw and understood his setups could get into the flow pretty easily. From just one setup, you could anticipate what he'd want to shoot next and always be ready for him. One of the best things that came from watching how Huell executed his vision of a story was that you could suggest shots that could serve as a bridge (or cover his narration), and he would actually listen to your ideas. Better yet, if he knew that you shared his vision, he'd be more likely to take the suggestion, and we'd shoot it.

Huell's style of shooting was also more cost effective, as he wasn't overutilizing the engineers for the shoot or the editing. When he came back from a shoot, everything we needed was all there, so the story could be edited in only a few hours. The videotape editors loved him. Pretty soon, it seemed that Huell was doing all the *Videologs*.

I loved to shoot for Huell and was always happy to see my name next to his on the assignment sheet. In fact, it was my work on one of the *Videolog*s I shot for Huell that inspired him to ask me to be his cameraman on *California's Gold*.

Huell and Luis at the original KCET campus in Hollywood.

Our Backgrounds

HUELL'S EARLY YEARS

If you're reading this, I figure you'd like to know something right off the bat about Huell. So here's a little bit about his upbringing, where he came from, and the path he set out on that brought him to KCET, where he and I would eventually meet.

Huell Burnley Howser came into the world on October 18, 1945, in Gallatin, Tennessee, a small town northeast of Nashville, America's country music capital. His parents were Harold and Jewell Howser, who combined their first names to come up with the unique name they gave their son. He and his sister, Harriett, enjoyed a happy and adventurous childhood, what he called an idyllic life. Their parents traveled with them often, and during the Christmas holidays, they'd take Huell and Harriett to New York City, where they saw Broadway plays and skated at Rockefeller Center. From an early age, Huell was exposed to people and places that were far outside of the experiences he knew growing up in a small town.

After his high school graduation, Huell joined the Marine Corps, and from there he got involved in politics. He started as an aide in Howard Baker's 1966 successful campaign for the Senate and later

The Howser family.

Huell in the Marine Corps.

became a member of Baker's Senate staff. After enrolling at the University of Tennessee at Knoxville, Huell wasted no time getting into campus politics. He also wrote for the school newspaper, and in his columns he had opinions on just about anything and everything that could affect students. From an unfair parking situation around campus to his thoughts about the Vietnam War, Huell always had a lot to say.

Huell wasn't going straight through college, and his father wasn't happy with his son's meandering path. He once told me that his dad had said, "Huell, you're going to have to get off this gravy train and do something with your life. You need to get out into the real world." The path that would lead to his real world came to him by chance.

In 1970, when he was twenty-five, Huell appeared on Nashville's *Noon* show on WSM-TV, promoting the student outreach group he'd helped create called *U-T Today* at the university. Huell did well in front of the cameras, explaining his story with passion and ease. The station's president was so impressed by the young man's appearance and on-camera personality that he hired him to work on documentary programs. From what I've heard, he told everyone that Huell was going to be a huge star someday.

Later that year, Huell went on television for the first time as the host for a series called *Rap On*. That show did well and led to another assignment, doing man-on-the-street interviews about the 1970 Tennessee governor and senate races. This was his first time in the out-of-studio interviewing business, and the segment was such a hit with viewers that it got him hired as one-fourth of a team of reporters on WSM-TV's nightly news.

WSM's president apparently had a real eye for spotting and hiring talent, because at the station, Huell also worked with John Tesh, a news anchor there from 1975 to '76 who went on to become not only a TV and radio star, but also a world-renowned composer. Another well-known guy who worked with Huell at WSM was *Wheel of Fortune*'s Pat Sajak, who was an announcer and did the weekend weather from 1974 to '77.

Huell at WCBS in New York. • *Opposite*: Dolly Parton, Huell, and Loretta Lynn.

It was at WSM-TV that Huell developed his familiar, easy style, producing and hosting short segments known as "Happy Features." Huell covered just about everything of interest, from quilting bees to a trip to the Middle East, and he interviewed such celebrities as Paul McCartney, Burt Reynolds, Dennis Weaver, and the Jackson Five. He had such a marvelous interview with Dolly Parton at her high-rise apartment overlooking Central Park in New York that you would have thought they were old high school friends. His unique style was truly disarming, friendly, and engaging, and he didn't let celebrity and fame get in his way when asking for interviews.

In 1979, after almost ten years at WSM-TV, Huell left the Nashville station and journeyed to New York City to work at WCBS-TV, the CBS flagship station. He'd hit the big time. In November of that year, he launched his own half-hour weekly newsmagazine show called *Real Life*. The style was about the same as in the features he'd become known for in Memphis. The name of the series was changed to *To Life* a month later, and it ran until it was canceled a year later.

Television has a way of doing that—changing the name of a show and/or changing the set, hoping changes will both bring in and retain viewers, but ultimately, I guess, Huell's easygoing style just didn't quite fit into the fast-paced New York City life.

Huell then accepted a job with Cable News Network (CNN) in Los Angeles as a reporter and relocated to the West Coast, beginning work in November of 1980. In 1981 he left CNN and began working as a feature reporter at KCBS-TV in LA. During that year, NBC also hired him to do a pilot for a new show called *Wedding Day*. He was teamed up with Mary Ann Mobley, a popular television actress who'd appeared on *Burke's Law* in the 1960s, as well as on *Fantasy Island, Perry Mason,* and many other shows. I'd guess that the former Miss America from Mississippi must have meshed pretty well with the Tennessean.

The idea behind the show called for Mary Ann and Huell to film

Huell with Mary Ann Mobley on *Wedding Day*.

and follow a couple around on their wedding day, including the actual ceremony. The pilot went on the air but, unfortunately, wasn't picked up. It could have been that the show was ahead of its time; I'm sure it would have fit better in today's reality show world. Whatever the reason, it didn't sell, and Huell went back to Tennessee, perhaps to regroup after the failure. Fortunately for us, Hollywood beckoned him once again, and he returned to California.

Huell went back to KCBS-TV (Channel 2) and continued doing feature reporting. In 1987, while still at Channel 2, he also began working for LA-based public broadcasting station KCET as a part-time producer on *Videolog*. It was for this series in 1988 that Huell produced the now-famous story of the reunion of elephant trainer Charlie Franks and Nita, the elephant he had given to the San Diego Wild Animal Park when Charlie retired from the circus. (You'll read more about that in a couple of chapters.) The popularity of that feature inspired KCET to ask Huell to expand *Videolog* into half-hour specials, which he did. These were critically acclaimed by *Los Angeles Times* television critic Howard Rosenberg, who wrote that each show was an "intimate, magnificently un-slick, utterly charming, absolutely irresistible half hour that is Howser at his populist best, just meeting common folk and letting them be themselves."

California's Gold was barely below the horizon.

MY EARLY YEARS

Now that you know something about Huell and where he came from before we met at KCET, I thought you'd want to know something about me—the guy named Louie on the *California's Gold* team whom you knew only by name. So here's a bit of my story. You'll see it's pretty much the opposite of the well-to-do nature of Huell's life, yet I believe that life has been generous to me, giving me one of the main things that I guess we all want in life: having a job that you love.

I was born on June 10, 1941, in San Bernardino, California—a work-ingman's city about sixty miles east of Los Angeles. My dad came to America from Mexico City as a young boy, and my mom was born in Riverside, just down the freeway from San Bernardino. My mother cleaned homes, and my father worked as a machinist at the Santa Fe railroad maintenance shops in San Bernardino.

I was the first of four children, with a younger brother and two sisters. My grandmother lived with us, and she and I spent a lot of time together. Tita spoke Spanish, and out of respect for her, that was the primary language we spoke at home. But in the neighborhood, with the kids, and at school, I picked up English and spoke it everywhere else outside the home.

When I was growing up in the 1950s, the music we listened to at home was mostly Spanish. When I was out of the house with my friends, however, we'd listen to the new rock and roll—but even back then, my preference for music was classical.

I absolutely loved classical music. Where my love for it came from, I'm not certain, but it may have been sparked by some of the classical music we played in the school band (I was on trumpet).

My brother also loved classical music. What were the odds of that—two brothers from the barrio digging Mozart and Bach? We shared a bedroom, and at night we'd tune our little radio to LA's classical music stations and be in heaven.

My dad was ambitious and hard working, and I admired him for that. He leased a grocery store in the nearby town of Colton while working full-time at the railroad shops, and when I was eleven, he put me to work as a meat cutter. I was something of a kid butcher, and I got pretty good at it—I still have all of my fingers. I was getting paid, so I didn't mind the work, although I can't say my father was paying me minimum wage. I had a goal for the money I made, and it seemed to take forever—but finally I saved enough to pay for what I really wanted: to become a Boy Scout.

I joined the Scouts and bought the uniform and everything else needed to be a Boy Scout in good standing. I really enjoyed the scouting life, so when I became too old for the Boy Scouts, I joined the Sea Scouts. I learned navigating skills, sailing, ropes, and pretty much everything essential to being a good seaman. I also began practicing long-distance ocean swimming, and was eventually certified as a lifeguard. When I graduated from high school in 1960, it seemed only natural to enlist in the Navy.

Boy Scout days.

Boot camp was a breeze for me, because I already knew all the stuff that the drill instructors were trying to cram into our hard, teenage heads. I did my tour of duty on a destroyer as a radarscope jockey, looking for planes and ships that could endanger our ship, and I'm happy to say I didn't spot a single hostile invader. It was just my luck that I was stationed in Hawaii—I mean, someone had to do it.

After two years, I left the Navy and enrolled at San Bernardino Valley College with the idea of becoming an electrical engineer. I also worked part-time at the nearby Lockheed plant to supplement my G.I. Bill benefits.

Has something ever come into your life out of the blue? Something that changed your life's direction and propelled you into unimagined opportunities—and you didn't have a speck of an idea about what it might be or when it would happen?

Well, that's exactly what happened to me.

I was on campus between classes with a friend who worked at the college television station. She said she'd like to take me on a tour to see the technical operations that went on behind television productions.

In the Navy.

We went into the studio, and I saw several television cameras parked across the floor.

I walked up to one and stood behind it, and from the very moment I touched it, I knew this was what I really wanted to do—I fell instantly in love with the camera. I wasted no time and changed my major to television engineering, learning each and every thing I could about the camera and the other engineering positions.

After college, I worked full-time at the Lockheed plant to pay for my schooling and to get the first-class licenses that were required in those days to do engineering work at radio and television stations. I got married in 1967, and in 1969, my daughter, Felicia, was born. My son, Michael, was born in 1974, and then I knew I had to head to LA to get a better-paying job.

Getting my first job in television was tough. For a year and a half, I made phone calls and drove all over Los Angeles and Hollywood for interviews. I got turned down or, even worse, heard what I thought were sincere, encouraging words that didn't result in a single callback.

Back then, getting a job in television had a lot to do with family relationships. There were a lot of father-son teams and uncles getting their nephews into the industry. (Yes, it was very male then.) But finally I got a call from a friend who worked as a cameraman at KCOP-TV (Channel 13) in Los Angeles. He said they needed a cameraman immediately, and he'd back me up with his boss. So I went over, got interviewed, and was hired on the spot. I probably wouldn't have heard about the job if my friend hadn't been there for me. Do I feel guilty that someone on the inside helped me? Not on your life. I look at it as a chance meeting with opportunity. Besides, we weren't related. The year was 1969, and my thirty- five-year career in television had begun.

Luis in the early television days.

In those days, KCOP was doing a lot of programs on location that we shot out of a wildly colored van, crammed to the roof with all kinds of gear. Guys from other stations would see us coming and they'd shout, "Here comes the circus truck!"

We shot boxing at the Olympic Auditorium and should have gotten hazardous-duty pay for doing camera work there. At the end of matches that featured a popular local boxer, we'd pay close attention to the ring announcer's reading of the fight scorecards. If the crowd favorite came out on the short end, we'd have to duck behind our cameras to avoid getting hit by flying objects. One thing's for sure: There was never a dull moment at the Olympic.

We also televised the Los Angeles Thunderbirds roller derby, which was memorable—not to mention fun. There was lots of action as guys and gals elbowed one another and sometimes tossed one another over the rail and into the audience. I learned how to move the camera on close-up action, with the skaters coming at my camera, and then following them as they sped away on the rink—all the while staying in focus on the skaters.

We also shot live commercials with Cal Worthington, the famous car salesman who would come onto the set riding a camel, or perhaps a long-horned bull. He'd look into the camera and, with a straight face, tell the viewers very seriously that he'd like them to meet his dog, Spot. You'd never know what he'd come in with, and sometimes, the animals he brought were truly quite frightening. He'd tug in a tiger or a bear on a chain, and it would raise the hair on the back of my neck.

After three years at KCOP, I got into KABC (Channel 7) as a tape operator setting up videotapes for the programs. I quickly found out that I'd probably be stuck doing that same task for a long, long time before there was any chance to move up and become a cameraman. I didn't like the situation, but I had a family, and it was a job in television, so I did it.

But then, only a few days after I was hired, I got a call from KCET (Channel 28, LA's public TV station) asking if I was available. I'd nearly forgotten that I had applied to work there. I almost bit my tongue saying, "Yes, yes, I'm available." I quit KABC, and the next day I started working at KCET—the station that eventually would become Huell Howser's home base. The year was 1972. I didn't know it at the time, but my life was about to change in ways I never could have imagined.

KCET'S
GOLDEN AGE
OF TELEVISION

I arrived at KCET at the beginning of its golden age of television production. I was lucky enough to have the opportunity to not only hone my craft but also to participate in creating some of the most innovative programs of the time. We all felt the excitement of being a part of the grand experiment.

Management at KCET wasn't afraid to experiment with productions, and they encouraged producers and writers to create shows that the commercial stations either wouldn't or couldn't touch. *Hollywood Television Theater* fit that description to a tee.

The Broadway and stage shows that comprised *Hollywood Television Theater* were often edgy and sometimes controversial, but they were always interesting to watch. I think that's what attracted a lot of great actors who wanted to work in television but also wanted to do something different. We were lucky that most of the talent was already working in Hollywood, so we had access to such remarkable actors as Keir Dullea and Richard Chamberlain. We shot a controversial show called *Steambath*, with Bill Bixby and Valerie Perrine, in which she briefly appeared nude. The towel she wore kept slipping off until some

The KCET campus in Los Feliz (photo by D. Converse).

brain came up with the idea to duct-tape it to her body—much to the disappointment of the engineers.

KCET also produced Carl Sagan's *Cosmos*, which featured a futuristic spaceship designed by art director John Retsek, and Steve Allen's *Meeting of Minds*, in which actors playing historical figures discussed and debated ideas and events. Allen's wife, Jayne Meadows, appeared as Marie Antoinette and Marie Curie, among many other historical characters.

We also shot a ton of remote productions that were unique to both KCET and to the television landscape at that time. From LA's Dorothy Chandler Pavilion one Sunday afternoon, we celebrated the arrival of Italy's Carlo Maria Giulini (the new conductor and music director of the Los Angeles Philharmonic) with a live broadcast of Beethoven's Ninth Symphony. Taylor Hackford, who later directed the blockbuster movie *An Officer and a Gentleman*, shot a marvelous opening segment in which the soft-spoken Maestro Giulini was introduced to his orchestra and began rehearsing. Those of us in the crew even wore tuxedos so we'd fit in with the crowd, and I think we looked pretty spiffy.

The Greek Theater in Griffith Park was one of our favorite places to shoot. It was a small venue with an intimate feel, and I think that came across on camera. Of the many programs we shot there, two of the most memorable were the Gipsy Kings and a marvelous retrospective of Agnes de Mille's innovative dance creations.

But KCET'S golden age might not have happened if it hadn't been a community-based station that got a little help from our union. Compared to the commercial stations, the technical staff was small, so the engineers' union allowed KCET's engineers to work in different jobs as needed on different productions—unlike commercial stations, which largely pigeonholed engineers into doing just one job. We could work lighting on one show, run camera on the next, and do other production jobs as they came up. This unique cross-training gave me opportunities to learn my favored craft as cameraman, but I also learned how to light both sets and people properly, and how to edit videotape and work sound. I was grateful for all of these learning opportunities, especially when doing camera work in the field, where I felt most comfortable and useful.

However, the learning at KCET wasn't all positive; it did come with some pain now and then as I was coming up through the ranks. For example, there were a few times that I did something wrong, and I *really* heard about it. The blunder that stands out the most is when we shot one of my favorite operas, *La Gioconda*, at San Francisco's famous opera house.

My camera sat high up in the balcony so I could get a full shot of the stage, and the audience was seated all around me. The great television director Kirk Browning led the shoot, and I was having a ball listening to him sing and hum along with the opera through the headphones. He sang me into the shots, setting me up and leading me to the next, following the beautiful music and voices as the opera unfolded. The act ended, the curtain closed, and I sat back from the camera, taking a break from the production. People came over to talk, curious about what I was doing. One man walked in the front of the camera and peered right into the lens. What I didn't know was that my camera was still hot—meaning it was recording and its picture going out live on the air.

To make matters worse, I had taken off my headset and couldn't hear the screaming and cursing in the control room ordering me to get that man's face out of the camera. Let me tell you, I heard an earful about that, and I felt bad for a long, long time. That was what I like to call the lesson from hell, but from then on, I made sure my camera was secured.

That mistake did not get in the way of the show, however, and all the engineers (including me) received a national Emmy for our work. Whew! To this day, it's sitting proudly on my fireplace mantel.

It was during this time that I started working on *Videolog*, which was the key for my eventual work on *California's Gold*. Taped on location, the very short shows were shot by the host, a cameraman, and a sound man, who was tethered to the cameraman and had to both carry a tape recorder and hold the microphone on a boom. It was an awkward way to shoot, with the three of us dancing around, trying to get the job done while staying out of each other's way. A big break came when an audio recorder was miniaturized and fitted into the camera, eliminating the sound man altogether and allowing for a more compact production unit. The team was now only two people: a host like Huell in front of the camera, and a cameraman like me behind it. It was the beginning of a new style of production that gave Huell the freedom to shoot all kinds of situations he couldn't before, and I believe it opened up almost limitless possibilities for his creativity.

Working with Huell as a two-man team on *Videolog* allowed me to combine all the technical experience I'd gotten at KCET in camera work, lighting, sound, and editing. From the moment Huell asked me to be his cameraman on *California's Gold*, I felt I was prepared to shoot for him, and would do a good job in recording the vision he had for the program. All of these disciplines came together with Huell's original and inimitable style to create the look and feel of *California's Gold* that so many love to this day.

NITA & THE GENESIS OF CALIFORNIA'S GOLD

Perhaps the most famous (and touching) *Videolog* story was from early 1989, a story we fondly referred to as "The Elephant Man." The segment was about a frail, eighty-year-old gentleman named Charlie Franks, who had been an elephant trainer in the circus. One of the elephants he'd trained and worked with became his favorite. He had acquired her in 1955 when she was only five years old and named her Nita. He traveled and performed with Nita all over the world and treated her with great care, affection, and admiration.

After he retired, Charlie arranged for Nita to go to the San Diego Wild Animal Park. Huell found out about Nita, recognized a story when he heard one, and he thought the best way to shoot it was to ask Charlie to accompany him to the park and interview him there. Charlie had not seen Nita for fifteen years. We drove down to the park and set up our gear so Huell could interview Charlie just outside the elephant enclosure. Huell sat and talked with Charlie, asking him questions about his career as a trainer and his years with Nita.

Huell then asked Charlie if he thought Nita would recognize him after not having seen him for more than fifteen years. Charlie got up slowly and, using his cane, ambled over to the edge of the elephant

enclosure. He paused and looked at Huell, and then he turned and called to a group of elephants some twenty-five yards away. In a playful voice, he said, "Nita, what are you doing out there? Nita, come here. Nita, you better get over here!" One of the elephants picked up its head, stepped back, and began looking around, searching for the source of the familiar voice. Charlie continued coaxing her to come over to him—even telling her he had a surprise for her—and at last, Nita left the herd and lumbered over. She stopped at the edge of the enclosure and extended her trunk. Charlie took it in his hand and caressed it, reassuring her that, indeed, it was he who had come to visit her after so much time apart. He fed her some jelly beans (one of her favorite treats, according to Charlie), and you could just see how fond these two were of each other. Their reunion touched me deeply, and I felt a lump in my throat as I ran the camera to capture this tender scene.

Huell also wanted to know if Nita would remember the old circus routines, and I think Charlie was just as curious. So he took charge, as if he were in the center ring once again. He instructed Nita through her act, and she performed each and every trick. She had not forgotten her routine, nor had she forgotten the man who had taught her. Toward the end of the show Huell asked about their special relationship, and with damp eyes, Charlie said, "You get attached to them... you just don't know when it happens."

When Huell asked if he thought he'd ever see Nita again, Charlie said that this was the last time; he felt that he was in such poor health that he wouldn't be able to make another trip. The emotional piece ended with Charlie saying his last goodbye to Nita. The gentle old man walked to the edge of the enclosure and, once again, reached his hand out to Nita. She extended her trunk and appeared to not just feel his hand, but to explore it for a while. As he walked away, she waved goodbye with her trunk. Charlie died less than a year later.

Looking back, I can only say that the story was told lovingly

Huell, Charlie, and Nita.

Nita and Charlie's emotional reunion captured on camera by Luis.

and with undeniable tenderness. It was hard to watch it unfold with dry eyes, and I believe that only Huell could have told it so well for television. It was at that shoot that I recognized his talent for reaching into people's hearts so they'd tell their stories with joy, wonder, and, at times, sadness. His disarming friendliness and genuine interest in people, coupled with his talent for asking the right questions, were the keys to getting people to open up and talk. These qualities would result in the artful construction of his future shows, which made them more than just interesting—they were unforgettable. At this early *Videolog* shoot, I got an early look at how Huell was becoming a master storyteller.

Although "The Elephant Man" was not a *California's Gold* show, it still ranks as one of my favorite shoots with Huell. Not only did the video come out well, but Huell told the heartwarming story with great simplicity and care. He had captured a moment that could not be repeated, the final parting of two old friends. And I was proud to be a part of it.

Getting the Nita story had been a stroke of luck; my name just happened to come up on the schedule for that day, and the scheduler teamed me up with Huell and the sound man (at that time, we worked old-style, in three-person shoots). We ended up creating a memorable piece of television that continues to stand out as a marker of how to tell a great story.

After that show, I worked with Huell many times on *Videolog* shoots, as did numerous other KCET staff cameramen. Beyond the professional relationship of producer and cameraman, we were easy and comfortable with each other, and we always had fun working together. Seeing Huell's shoots next to my name on the schedule assignment made me happy because I knew we'd be doing something interesting— and I knew I could give him the footage he wanted.

About a year after "The Elephant Man" show, Huell and I were out on a two-man *Videolog* shoot. We had wrapped up and were headed back to the KCET studio. Huell was behind the wheel, where he liked to be, but he wasn't talking much about the shoot like we usually did. He seemed preoccupied. Finally, he turned to me and said he was thinking about doing a new show. He had an idea of doing a program using a two-man crew, just a cameraman and himself, like we did on *Videolog*.

I recall tentatively saying, "Yeah...?" He said the hook was that he and the cameraman would travel throughout California, visiting interesting places, meeting interesting people, and getting into California history. That angle appealed to me, as I'm a bit of a history buff.

He envisioned the program as a series of thirteen half-hour shows annually, shot over a period of ten years. That seemed to me to be one heck of a schedule projection. But Huell already had ten years in his head, and when he put his mind to something, you just knew it was going to work out—talk about confidence and vision. I was already impressed with the way he produced his stories, and the project seemed to be a natural fit for him, so I said it sounded like a great idea. He said he'd begun to make presentations to get funding for the series, and he thought he had a good shot at getting the money.

Then he told me he'd talked to another cameraman at KHJ-TV about doing the show, but nothing had been finalized. I didn't ask, but I assumed their deal had been put on hold because Huell didn't have funding yet, and the show was going to air on a non-commercial station, so money might be tight. The cameraman would have to quit his job and take a chance on Huell's idea becoming a success on public television.

We were on Sunset Boulevard, close to the KCET lot, when Huell turned to me and asked if I would like to be the cameraman if the funding went through. I didn't give it a second thought. I said, "Yeah, I'll do it."

That's how I got hired to be the cameraman on *California's Gold*: a show that was still up in the air, really just an idea, but that would go on to become one of the most beloved public television programs in the country.

And it all started with Nita and Charlie.

CALIFORNIA'S GOLD
TAKES SHAPE

When I accepted his offer to work on *California's Gold*, Huell explained the deal in greater detail. For starters, I'd be working on the show full-time for a year, and he'd pay me directly through his program's budget. He also said I'd have to ask KCET what it thought about me leaving to work directly for Huell. I said I would, but added that we should wait until he got the series funded. Huell agreed, but I could see he was confident that I'd be talking with management soon.

The big questions filling my mind were about my medical benefits and seniority at the station—protecting my family was my number-one priority. If the funding went through, would KCET give me a one-year leave of absence and allow me to keep my medical benefits? Would the station (and the union) let me keep my seniority? Would KCET and the union go for a deal that would be completely new to them?

I was in the field operations office one day when Huell dropped by. He sat in the chair across the desk from me and leaned forward with a small grin on his face. In a cool voice, he asked if I remembered that I'd have to take a leave of absence from KCET for a year. I said, "Yes, I recall that." Then he asked if I was ready to do the show we had talked about.

It finally hit me: I asked if he had gotten the funding, and he smiled all big and said, "Yes, I got the money from Wells Fargo, and we're ready to go." I reached out and shook his hand and congratulated him. I was excited! We were going to do his new show all over California—if I could get it past the chiefs. I told him I'd discuss the deal with management at the station and with the union, and he told me to get it done as soon as I could, because he was ready to get out there and shoot.

A man lesser than Huell may not have been able to pull off getting funding for the show. I don't remember exactly when, but later I learned that Wells Fargo had made a stipulation in the contract that required Huell to get all thirteen California public broadcasting stations to agree to air it before they'd turned over the money. Huell took on that task on his own, driving up to Eureka and working his way down the state to visit all the PBS stations. At each station, he pitched his idea about doing a series on California and its many wonders, and every single one of them agreed to put the show on the air. He took the agreements to Wells Fargo, and the bank released the funds.

I followed up quickly on my part of the bargain. I talked with my boss, the chief engineer, and he said it was fine with him. KCET's management liked Huell's program concept and was enthusiastic about me shooting the program, so they gave the go-ahead for the leave of absence and allowed me to keep my medical benefits and union seniority. I was so relieved that things had gone my way without a hitch.

WE GET TO WORK

It was now the second half of 1990, and Huell and I were ready to start on the first *California's Gold* episode. About three weeks after we had finalized the deal, I was on the lot in the engineers' office when Huell's secretary called. We exchanged pleasantries and then she said, "Louie, Huell wants you to come and pick up the Ford Explorer and take it in to get it serviced."

I sat up in my chair and said, "What?"

She repeated what she had said about getting the car serviced. I asked her for the direct number to Huell's office and hung up.

I called and Huell picked up.

I said, "Huell, what's this? Your secretary says you want me to take your car to get serviced?"

He said, "Well, Louie, it's not *my* car. It's really *our* car, the one we'll be using to drive all over California when we shoot."

I said, "Huell, I'm sorry but you know that car is not parked in *my* driveway at *my* home. You're going to have to make other arrangements to get the car serviced, because you hired me to do camera, sound, and lighting. If my not servicing your car is an issue, we may have to move on."

I got the feeling that something was going on at the other end because he didn't say anything for a while. I remember thinking that he was probably staring at his phone in disbelief, saying to himself, *Did Louie actually say that? Did I really hear him say that?*

I realized that he actually might call off our deal and fire me before we even rolled the camera on the first shoot.

He broke the silence, saying matter-of-factly, "Okay, I'll take it in."

He did, and he never once mentioned our little incident again.

That conversation helped set our boundaries. I think at that point he gained more respect for me as a person and as the show's cameraman, and I'd always had respect for him. That mutual respect permitted each of us the freedom to contribute the best of our individual talents to the shoots, and I think that's what made us so successful. I still believe the respect we had for each other allowed Huell to be comfortable and open with me, and in turn that helped our shooting to be seamless and creative.

When we were out shooting, I don't think he ever worried about how he was going to say something to me or how his words would affect me personally. Typically, when he told me what he wanted in a shot or setup, I felt like he'd left the door open for me to express my opinions. He wanted to know what I thought about how we should get the look he was after. That was respect. I couldn't have asked for more from Huell.

He could be strong and forceful at times, and I'd seen and heard Huell impose his will on others. I wasn't going to let him do that to me and affect my work. Knowing the technical end of things well, I had a good idea of what I could bring to the show, and I knew that he was exceptionally good at what he did on the other side of the camera. That was our dividing line, and this mutual respect held up for the twelve years we worked together.

Huell and I began shooting the first *California's Gold* in November of 1990, with a projected airdate in January. The schedule gave him more than enough time to edit (and perhaps re-edit) the show after we'd finished shooting. I think it was particularly interesting that the first show featured three segments shot in different parts of the state, which required a lot of travel time, and all three were as different from one another as night and day. I didn't really see any central theme or focus connecting them.

The first segment of that very first show was a story about a town near Sacramento called Locke, and the Chinese immigrants who settled there in the 1800s. For the second segment, we traveled to a small town just north of San Diego called Vista, where we shot an old-time tractor show. The concluding segment was a piece we shot in Banning, almost a hundred miles east of Los Angeles, that featured Native American songs by the Cahuilla Bird Singers.

I think Huell was influenced by *Videolog* (the short stories we shot that were shown in between regularly scheduled programs as fillers) when he decided on the organization of the first *California's Gold*. The three unrelated segments in that first show—a new series that prom-ised to show the wonders of California and its people—might have stemmed from a lack of confidence that he could hold the audience's attention with a single story. Or it may have been that he wanted to lead off the series with as many different California subjects as he could reasonably put in the half hour, perhaps to show the sponsor that he was, indeed, presenting California's diverse wonders. I always re-gret not asking him about that, because before long, the show settled into the form it was meant to have: a full thirty minutes devoted to one story theme or location.

The second *California's Gold* took place in and around San Luis Obispo. We shot at four locations: the mission, a place that claimed to be the world's first motel, a saloon that had been a former stagecoach stop, and the Dunitas, sand dunes on the coast just outside of town. To me, the segments didn't seem to have a lot in common, except for the fact we had shot them all in and around San Luis Obispo. I felt that Huell was going quickly from one place to another to try to move the show along and keep it interesting.

We shot the third episode, called "Lost Sierra", in a town called Downieville in the Sierra Nevada. Unlike the first and second episodes, which were purely location based, this one consisted of three segments tied together by the community's history and isolation.

The fourth *California's Gold* had only two segments: the first was about the Los Angeles Watts Towers, and the second took us to the Bay Area, where we shot a segment on San Francisco's sourdough bread. Huell may have felt that those two subjects were what the cities were famous for, but, personally, I thought if that was the theme of the show, he could have chosen subjects in each city that had something more concrete in common.

Show number five, which aired in May of 1991, was called "LA Ad-ventures," and we shot it all over Los Angeles. We shot so many dif-ferent stories that day: an old grapefruit tree in Little Tokyo that was

still bearing fruit, the La Brea Tar Pits, the famous arching Encounter Restaurant in the Theme building at LAX, Grand Central Market in downtown, and, finally, the buried bridge on the UCLA campus. Huell drove us all across town, and I shot him covering unrelated subjects that each lasted only a few minutes.

The sixth show seemed to be the turning point. Huell hit his well-known long form in the show called "Trains," which we shot at Railfair '91, located at the California State Railroad Museum in Sacramento. Huell got into a groove on the historic trains and was truly wowed by his discoveries. Even through the viewfinder of the camera, I saw that he was genuinely enthusiastic and at ease. He brought out his guests' love for trains, encouraging them to express their feelings, asking the right questions, and moving the show along. We ended with a train ride in a restored old locomotive through the scenic Mother Lode foothill country. The program flowed beautifully. I still don't know exactly what did it. Perhaps it was Huell acting like an excited little boy, playing with his trains and getting lost in them. Whatever it was, Huell had finally hit the *California's Gold* stride that you all know and love.

The following years, Huell and I shot hundreds of segments that captivated his audiences. Whatever and whomever we shot, Huell's take on them was always what the shows were about—his wonder and his perspective on people, events, and things. As he learned to relax and take his time with the material, the shows became more compelling. Huell seemed to be having more fun with his guests, and we began to see more of his remarkable gift for getting his guests to open up and tell us the one-of-a-kind stories that were simply amazing.

By then, Huell could do a whole show about a carrot and you wouldn't change the channel, because he made that root so darn interesting.

On location for the "Trains" episode.

From my perspective, Huell wanted only the bare minimum amount of information from his staff—just enough to know what the show was about and what he hoped to get from it. Otherwise, he wanted to learn the rest during interviews so he could make his discoveries on camera. His trademark phrases of, "Oh, wow!" "Golly!" "Oh, my gosh!" and "That's amaaazing!" followed by a friendly, "Louie, take a look at this!" were genuine, and you heard them more and more as we continued our work together. Yes, it's true that Huell's astonishment bar was set pretty low, but I believe his viewers and fans went along with this because they knew he was sincere in his love for his discoveries.

That was the real Huell; it was just a part of his style, and it was entirely genuine. There was a little Gomer Pyle in there, but it worked well for him. I don't think anyone else could have been as successful with the material as he was, with his small-town talk and inquisitiveness wrapped in a Southern drawl that played so unexpectedly well in big cities like Los Angeles and San Francisco.

If you take a good look at the show and the way it's structured, you'll notice that there's nothing fancy about the style of shooting we developed. The method was straightforward—really, just an extension of what we had done on the *Videolog* shows, except now Huell had the opportunity to do it in a longer form.

Huell used a couple of specific phrases to describe the look of *California's Gold* and the way we shot it. One was, "This ain't brain surgery." But his favorite phrase to say about the look of the show and his style of delivery was, "This isn't rocket science." I still remember the times I'd be setting up a shot, taking lots of time and probably overthinking it, when he'd walk up and give me the rocket-science bit. He was usually right, and I learned to love those words of wisdom.

Once he embraced the half-hour *California's Gold* format, Huell could really dig into a story, which allowed him to grow as a storyteller. Those short *Videolog*s were confining, and I think their limited length quashed his creativity. We all knew he had a lot more to say.

When he had exceptionally good material (for example, our Golden Gate Bridge shoot), Huell used the half hour to lay out a story with an exciting flow that kept viewers anticipating each new shot and each insightful bit of information.

As the show finally took shape into one thirty-minute story, I realized that the work really wasn't full-time. I had a lot of down time, because some months we only worked between six to ten days out of thirty. I wanted to keep working to keep my skills sharp, so I talked with Huell about the possibility of working on outside productions when we weren't shooting *California's Gold*. He agreed, but with the stipulation that he'd have first dibs on me when we had a show to shoot.

So during that first year, when I wasn't shooting *California's Gold*, I was staying busy as a freelancer doing all kinds of shows. Heck, I even got hired by KCET for other camera work. In that first year, KCET's scheduler (who knew my *California's Gold* schedule from Huell) put me to work when I was available, so I really never got completely away from the studio and the people I had worked with over the years.

At the end of the first year of filming, Huell and I sat down and talked about the shooting situation for the next year. We agreed that I should go back to KCET full-time, but with the same agreement; that he'd have first call on me when he needed me to do camera on *California's Gold,* as well as his other shows.

KCET management loved the show and the impressive ratings it was pulling in, so they went along with our plan and agreed to have me working as a full-time engineer on their productions, then loaning me out to Huell for the many shows he was doing. That deal between Huell, KCET, and me held together for the entire time I was shooting for Huell. The schedulers automatically assigned me to any show that had his name attached as producer. It was a win-win for all of us.

Shooting on the banks of the LA River.

OUR WORKING RELATIONSHIP

Huell and I had an excellent relationship that enabled us to work well together, and a lot of that resulted from the strong mutual trust we had in each other—but it took a little time to develop that in the field.

During our first few shoots, Huell would always end his interview (or whatever he was doing) by coming over to look at the monitor to see if I had gotten what he wanted. It was a cumbersome way to shoot— Huell would have to break to go back and forth, and I'd have to stop and hit replay to show him the images I'd taped.

It was his prerogative to check the tape, as he was both the field producer and the talent, but I couldn't help but find it irritating—it showed me that he lacked confidence in my ability to get the look he wanted. I had shot with him many times before on *Videolog,* and he knew my work well, but on the first few *California's Gold* shoots, he kept insisting on checking the tapes himself.

Eventually, he realized I knew how to deliver what he wanted to see, and he stopped breaking to come check my footage. Instead he would just smile, maybe nod his head, and purse his lips in satisfaction at what he'd just accomplished, and then we'd move on to the next thing.

In fact, once he finally allowed me to be the judge of the quality of the footage, he'd look at me after a take to see if I'd give him the nod that he'd done all right. He'd say, "What do you think, Louie? Did it look okay?" Of course, ninety-nine percent of the time it was right on. The show was his baby, and I was shooting it just as he had envisioned it.

On most shoots in the field, Huell knew what he wanted in a shot pretty much right away—and he was never afraid to tell me what he wanted. I'd check the spot he wanted to stand on, the sound and lighting situation, the background (to see how it would work in the frame), and then I'd set up and shoot. Sometimes, however, he'd have a harder time figuring out what to do, and he'd take some time trying to come up with the shot he wanted. (His line about *California's Gold* not being rocket science got thrown out the window like the proverbial baby with the bathwater!) He'd walk around and think, sizing up the options and possibilities. When he couldn't make up his mind, he'd finally ask my opinion: "How do you think we should shoot this, Louie?"

I'd ask what he was trying to achieve, or what he was looking for in the shot, and after he told me, I'd think about the layout, composition, and how he'd envisioned it, and I'd come up with a shot that I thought would work. Usually, he'd take me up on my idea and we'd shoot it as I saw it. He trusted me because he knew I could get the shot, and because he knew my suggestion was made with his vision in mind. We were there to tell the most interesting and well-shot stories we could, and our collaboration enabled us to do just that.

But every now and then, even after we'd talked about a shot and agreed to a particular plan, Huell didn't always follow through. He'd be holding a microphone with his guest, or setting up to make a comment about something, and I'd see him hesitate—his face reflecting the wheels turning in his head. I'd think, *Uh, oh—you're thinking about changing the shot. What are you going to do, Huell?*

Indeed he was rethinking the shot—rearranging or dismissing our previous plan, because he had gotten caught up in whatever new idea had just popped into his head. He'd change what he was going to do on the fly, and I'd get my camera and body ready to follow his moves, open to the possibilities, like a defensive back in a football game. He trusted me to adapt on the spot, and he knew I'd pick up his moves and cover him no matter what he did.

On one particular shoot in the Bay Area, my ability to be reactive and go with the flow was put to the test. We were doing a show about the Japanese Tea Garden in San Francisco, and Huell was completely unpredictable. He just loved that place, and he was as excited as a kid in a candy factory and zoomed around like a kid would. We'd talk about and set up a shot, and I'd begin to shoot him with his interview subject. Suddenly he'd spot something out of the corner of his eye and say something like, "Oh, look at that bridge!" and I'd have to quickly pan to it so the audience could see it. He wasn't giving me the usual slight head or foot movements that signaled a new direction; it was just arms and legs flying about and lunges at things that grabbed his attention. That's how the shoot went all day—yet, the show came out looking pretty good. Talk about a miracle.

If Huell was interviewing someone and decided to walk and talk with him or her, I'd go along, not questioning him or his actions because that's how he wanted me to shoot the show. He had the freedom to do something spontaneous, whatever came into his head, and he trusted that I would follow him to capture it, and for the most part, I did. There were times, however, that I'd be totally off in anticipating a move—I'd assume he was going to start walking, for instance, when I saw his feet or his body move, but in fact he had no intention of moving at all. Of course, I would have already started moving the camera in the direction I thought he'd be going. So there I'd be with egg on my face and a shot that was completely unusable. I'd stop the action, apologize, and reset the shot, and then Huell would tell me exactly what he was going to do—or not do—and we'd get a good shot on the next try.

Huell knew my goal was not only to get the right shot, but also to make him look good. I always checked the light, camera angle, background, and sound—everything that would frame him well, make him sound clear, and bring out the best in his look. He was the driver, the one who made the show and steered it, and the one who shared the unique, folksy personality that viewers loved so much. My job was to capture that, and I believe I did it well.

Huell's confidence in my preparation and technical ability allowed him the freedom to really get into telling the story. He didn't have to worry about any of the technical aspects, because I covered them all. He was then better able to concentrate on getting the best out of an interview subject or singing the praises of a place that impressed him greatly.

This mutual respect and open communication allowed me to sometimes pull Huell aside after we shot something and say, "Huell, what do you say we do this shot again, this other way?" I'd give him solid reasons that had nothing to do with technical or outside issues. Sure, we often had to stop shooting when we lost video or an airplane flew over or something else made a shot unusable, but in these cases, I'd be talking about a creative issue. I'd explain that, in my opinion, if we did it differently, the new shot would look better and make both him and the editor a heck of a lot happier when they were in the editing room. I'd explain how the story—his story—would flow more smoothly, and that aesthetically, it would look better on the screen. Huell would typically take me up on my suggestion, and we'd do another shot the way I'd suggested. I believe that deep down, he knew I'd parked my ego at the door and put the show first, and that I was truly focused on making him and the show look better. Most importantly, he knew that I looked at the show not only as the cameraman, but also as an editor who had the task of assembling the show.

For the most part, wherever we went throughout California, it was just the two of us—Huell as the host and me as his technician. A few times, on big shoots, a member of his staff would come along to assist with logistics, but for ninety-nine percent of the shows, Huell and I were the only team members. That close relationship helped me be straightforward with him, and helped him be open to me when I had to ring the bell.

LEARNING FROM EACH OTHER

As we did our *California's Gold* shoots, I studied Huell's actions, his mannerisms, the way he moved, his way of talking, and how he got people to relax and get into what they really wanted to talk about—as easily as if he was an old friend hanging out in their kitchen, chatting over a cup of coffee. I marveled at his natural talent.

Even though much of what Huell did made the shoots flow well, sometimes he'd unintentionally get in his own way. When we first started, for instance, he'd turn to the camera and say, "I like that, I really like that," as soon as he finished an interview. He might have done that on our shoots for *Videolog* (I don't remember), but because the shoots were so short and would be on the air for only a few minutes, it wouldn't have been an issue. But now we were shooting half-hour shows, and the video needed to have continuity and points at which the editor could cut, to go from one angle to another or perhaps to get us into another scene. When Huell said, "I like that" immediately after an interview, it made it hard for the editor to cut properly.

After a few shoots with him saying that (and me wincing every time), I finally put my camera down and walked toward Huell, gesturing for him to meet me halfway so his interviewee wouldn't be in on the conversation. Gently, I said, "Huell, please, when you're done with your interview, either walk away or just look at the camera and stop; just hold the mic and stop talking while I roll the camera. I'll know when to stop shooting. If you do that, you'll give your editor an edit point so he can use as much of the tape as he thinks looks good before he cuts to the next shot. Otherwise, you're going to drive him crazy, and he's going to want to kill me for letting you get away with it—and, I tell you, that won't work for me." He listened and took my advice well, under-standing that I was only trying to make him and the show look better. He never again said how much he liked the shot. It doesn't take much to make me happy.

Something else we developed that worked well for us was setting up good lighting. Early on I told him, "Huell, when I'm shooting and I start moving around, watch me out of the corner of your eye. If you see me moving it's because I want you to move, so the lighting hits you properly." So if he was in the middle of an interview and saw me moving, maybe circling him a bit, he'd start subtly moving the person around to adjust for the best light, without breaking the flow of the interview at all. We got very good at it—the interviewees had no idea.

The next time you see a *California's Gold* interview with me work-ing the camera, just watch his eyes and see how we both move. I kind of liken it to a classical music performance in which the musicians are playing the music on their stands while also watching the conductor's moves, keeping to his tempo, seeing where he's placing his attention, and reacting to him to keep the music moving in concert.

Huell was ever the showman, and he knew he was a celebrity up and down California. Whenever there was a crowd, even just two or three people, Huell was on. I'd fall back and leave him to the adulation of his fans, and he loved the attention. But there was one situation that came up on a five-day shoot in Yosemite when his celebrity status got to him and pushed him over the top.

I was setting up my lighting and camera equipment for a shoot in-side the majestic Ahwahnee Hotel. Huell and I were talking about what he wanted when a crowd of people walked in and spotted him. They rushed over, shouting, "Huell, Huell, Huell!" As they gathered around him, someone asked what we were doing, and he said we were setting up for an interview. Then, out of the blue, he turned and waved his hand around the big room and with great authority said, "Louie, put a light over here and another over there, and we'll set up the interview right over here." I really think he expected me to follow through with a "Yessir, right away, sir!" and put those lights here and there to his specifications. But I didn't. I was hot under the collar.

I walked over, took him by his elbow, and urged him away from the crowd. When we were out of earshot I said firmly, "Huell, you don't tell me to put a light here and put a light there. I know you got carried away putting on a show for your fans, but you don't tell me what to do with the lighting. I know how to light correctly. And if you think you do have to give me instructions on lighting, tell me what kind of lighting you want. Character lighting, soft lights, hard lights—whatever you want, I'll set it up."

Huell appeared to think hard about my little speech, about the many possibilities involved in lighting the interview for best effect. Then he looked at me out of the corner of his eye, clicked his tongue in his cheek, and said sheepishly, "Oh, Louie, just do whatever you want." I said, "Thank you very much, sir," and he went back to his fans while I set up the lights as close as I could to the spots he had pointed to. I had my responsibilities. But he never again told me how to light a set. We really did learn from each other as we grew into the series, and as we both got better at our craft, it all came together to create the look and feel of *California's Gold* that you all know.

As you've seen so many times in the programs, Huell possessed remarkable storytelling abilities, and he had an innate talent for pulling a great story from whomever he was interviewing. We always discussed the story we were going to shoot and what he was looking for as we traveled to our destination, and most of time I had a pretty good handle on what he wanted before we started shooting. But really, the stories were mostly in his head.

After we'd worked on several shows together, I realized that he was steering and constructing stories as we shot, and then filling in any blanks he thought were needed to make the stories work. That takes a special talent. Think of it—he's interviewing someone he doesn't know, has never seen before, and he's not very familiar with the story they're going to tell. And yet, on an instinctive level he knew what he wanted in his head, and most of the time he got the story moving exactly where he wanted it to go.

That doesn't mean he wasn't open to discoveries and new directions. If he chanced upon something that seemed to be more interesting than his original concept, we'd go there instead. The things he found interesting were the things he believed his audience would enjoy, and indeed they did. He always had his viewers in mind as we worked, and by observing him, I learned so much about how to build a story. He showed me that all good stories, no matter how long or how short, have a beginning, middle, and end. They follow a sequence as they build and then reconcile themselves in the end. I don't know if Huell ever really had to think about those things as he told his stories—he was just a marvelous natural storyteller, so the elements fell into place beautifully.

Huell taught me the art of storytelling, and that made me a better cameraman. He showed me that a story must have a hook at the beginning, something to grab your initial interest, and then deliver that promise as it unfolds. His intro at the top of each show created the interest both visually and verbally by laying out what you were going to experience, and from him, I learned how to build the story from that beginning.

KEEPING IT PROFESSIONAL

My relationship with Huell was completely professional. We didn't socialize outside of work, and we pretty much set that pattern up from the moment we started working together.

Huell was gregarious—he loved to be around people and schmooze, and after a shoot he'd often meet up for a drink with people who'd been in the show we were shooting. He liked to party—that was his nature, to be with people, talk with them, and have a good time.

I, on the other hand, am more quiet and reserved, and I wasn't accustomed to all the attention that came about during our shoots. Perhaps those differences helped make the show work so well—we didn't have the competing egos that might have harmed the shows as a result of a clash of personalities. It may very well be true that opposites attract, because our personalities and talents dovetailed so well.

After the first few shoots, we ate together at the end of the day, enjoying a meal and talking about the day's work and what we were going to do the next day if it was a multi-day shoot. When we finished work, we'd go to our hotel to clean up, and he'd call me in my room and say, "Louie, I'll be down in ten minutes and we'll go eat somewhere." Well, ten minutes would turn into a half hour or an hour. I gave him some rope, but eventually I realized that this wasn't going to work. I finally said, "Look, once we're done shooting, why don't we go our separate ways? I can clean the gear and get set up for the next day, get something to eat, and keep track of my expenses, and you can do what you want." I knew that while I was waiting for him to be ready to eat dinner, he was working on the show, talking with people on the phone or in person, but I needed to eat and then have time to unload my equipment, label tapes, clean my camera, and prep the gear for the next day's shooting. So for the rest of our time working together, we'd say a friendly goodbye after a good day's work and go our separate ways for dinner.

We were completely dependent on the batteries in the field, so in the evenings I had to make sure they were fresh and fully recharged. I'd have a beer or two while I did my work, after which I'd shower, find a place to have dinner, go back to my room, call my wife to check in and see how things were going, and be in bed by nine o'clock. My routine sounds pretty dull and uneventful as I describe it now, but it worked well for me (and the show) because I'd be rested, prepped, and ready for the next day's shooting.

Once in a while, Huell would ask me to go to dinner or a meeting with people who were in the program we were shooting, usually to add my two cents about technical stuff, and of course I'd go and enjoy it. But after that I'd head back to my room and settle into my routine. Most of the time I didn't know what Huell did after a shoot, or when he eventually went to bed, but a few times I could see that he hadn't slept much.

We didn't talk much when we were on the road. We'd exchange pleasantries and then he'd tell me about the show, the location, and whatever else I might need to know about the upcoming shoot. Usually, I'd just ask questions of a technical nature and then silently run a mental inventory of the gear I'd brought to make sure I had the right stuff to shoot the show the way he envisioned it. Huell liked to drive and was usually at the wheel of the Ford Explorer, so after we got our business talk out of the way, I'd lean back in my seat, shut my eyes, and sleep until we arrived, or until it was time for a pit stop. Most of the time, whether Huell was driving or I was, we didn't even listen to the radio. On occasion, Huell would listen to talk shows or classical music, but usually it was a quiet time so one of us could catch a nap.

I got to know his moods and could tell when he was up or down, usually by his tone of voice, and I could always tell when he was preoccupied with something. Depending on what I could read from his manner, I'd either chat with him, or just lie back and keep my mouth shut until he started up a conversation.

Whenever we traveled by air to get to our shoots, we'd fly on the same plane, but he'd sit up front and I'd be buried somewhere in the back with the big camera (which I did not let out of my sight), so, naturally, we didn't really talk on the flight. I think he liked being up front, where he could entertain his fellow passengers.

That was just the way it was. I was the technician and he was the star. The mutual respect we had for each other—and our respective positions—was the backbone of our relationship, and it allowed us to work so well together for so many years. My job was to make him look good and sound good, and I believe that from the technical side, the quality of my work matched his.

Now, I'm not saying I was the best in my profession—in fact, I guarantee there were better cameramen than me. But something about the fit between the two of us, Huell and me, was just the right combination to make *California's Gold* a lasting and wonderful series.

Early days shooting in front of the trusty Ford Explorer.

HOW WE SHOT
CALIFORNIA'S GOLD

You should know that to make *California's Gold*, we had neither scripts nor location scouts. Huell and I were the only members of the team, and we were the first ones to walk onto the shoot site every single time. We didn't have a sheet that told us the best places to set up, or what shots were absolutely must-haves—we decided all that once we saw it for ourselves.

What we did have were photos, brochures, and newspaper clippings, as well as names and telephone numbers of the people we were going to interview. So we knew the important things about the fair, or the mine, or the island we were visiting, and we knew the basics about why we were there. But beyond that, we didn't know much, and we were typically hundreds of miles from home. Yet I never worried—I knew Huell could deliver on his end and we'd get a good show.

When we'd arrive at the production site, we'd start by meeting with the people whom Huell was going to interview. He'd ask some questions based on the information he had in hand, but he did not pre-interview them. He liked to do things on the fly, making it up as we went along to keep the show spontaneous. Sometimes, while talking to the person he was supposed to interview on tape, someone more interesting would pop up, so we'd shoot that person instead—we were always flexible.

After talking with the interviewees, we'd walk around the area looking for the best places to shoot, and then we'd sit down and plan the shooting script that would best show our viewers why Huell chose to feature the place. He wanted to make the stories so compelling and enchanting that you'd feel bad for the rest of your life if you didn't go visit the place.

We'd talk about how to implement his ideas with the camera shots, what he wanted to shoot first, what he thought was important to cover, and how he wanted to open the episode. I'd go over his shooting ideas to see how I could set up the lighting and sound, and, of course, to see how interesting and creative the shots could look. Then we'd set up and begin shooting.

From the early days of shooting *Videolog*, I saw Huell's gift for interviewing people, but it wasn't until we were well into shooting *California's Gold* that I understood how essential this was to his storytelling success. He was a master at bringing out the best in people. His overwhelming friendliness and folksy demeanor put people at such ease that their stories would just come spilling out. He showed excitement about even the smallest things, and that encouraged people to open up to him and forget about being nervous in front of a camera. They saw that he was genuine and that he was truly fascinated by them.

Every shooting situation was new to us, so we had nothing to fall back on and nothing to hang our shooting hats on. But there was always one common thread, and that's what made the process work so well: Huell's charm and personality. He worked his magic every time. When we left a shoot to go home, we'd be waving goodbye to friends, not just random people we'd just interviewed.

As I shot each video, I listened intently to the conversation that Huell was having with his interview subject. I used that information to go on after the interview and shoot what's called the "B roll," footage that the editor would cut into the story to make it work visually.

For instance, take the show about farmers' roadside fruit and vegetable stands in the San Joaquin Valley. Huell and the farmers talked about the quality and seasonality of various fruits and vegetables. After we wrapped the interviews, I walked around and got close-up footage of the beautiful produce. The editor cut to those shots while Huell did the voiceover interview, so you could see the produce they were talking about.

A somewhat more dramatic example occurred when we were doing the episode about the St. George Reef Lighthouse, twelve miles off the Crescent City coast. We were taken out by helicopter, as that's the only way to get there. While we were hovering over the lighthouse, I said to Huell, "Let me go down in the basket first, and I'll get a shot of what it's like to go down to the lighthouse." I did my usual monkey-like one-arm hold while I rolled the tape from inside the helicopter's lowering basket and got the shot as I went down. When I was on the ground, I aimed the camera up to get a shot of Huell coming down in the basket.

Huell being dropped down from a helicopter above St. George Reef Lighthouse.

When you look at the sequence of shots in the show, you see him descending, and as he looks down, it cuts to a view of the ground coming up—what he is "seeing" as he descends. But, of course, it was actually what I was seeing. It made the show look like a bigger-budget two-camera shoot, and the editor got good material to work with.

I also asked the helicopter pilot to fly us around the island to give the viewers a good look at the rugged, sea-swept rock the lighthouse sat on. I tried to create visual interest with shots like those, so you'd get into the story and experience it through Huell's eyes. And I knew that those B-roll shots would make the editor deliriously happy.

Huell's style of storytelling was simple and straightforward, and that was a blessing for me as a cameraman. He didn't do anything fancy or outlandishly complicated that would have given me splitting headaches and perhaps cause me to utter foul language. If you really think about it, his storytelling style was remarkably similar to show-and-tell at school—but laced with tremendous and heartfelt enthusiasm.

That style of shooting may have been Huell's philosophy in general, but nonetheless, he'd sometimes still get us into tight, harrowing situations. One that stands out is the show from Santa Barbara Island. I was shooting Huell as he walked on a narrow trail perched on the edge of a cliff that plunged hundreds of feet down to the ocean. There I was, hoisting a very heavy camera while trying to keep Huell in the shot and watching where my own feet were going, thinking about what a slip would mean. I also remember following Huell as he talked into his mic while traversing a narrow walkway bordered by two pools of water in the ruins of the old Sutro Baths in San Francisco, as seen in the "California Pools" episode. Thank goodness those tough shots weren't regular occurrences—most shoots were far less dangerous. And most of the shot setups seemed to present themselves naturally. When we arrived at a new location, I'd quickly get the lay of the land and look for the most interesting spots for Huell and his guest to talk, always looking for how to frame them to best service the story. For instance, having Huell walk among—and gush about—the poppies at the Poppy Reserve (not far from Lancaster) was a natural fit for him and to tell that episode's story.

Huell and I also figured out our walking-while-shooting routine pretty early on, and it's something you see often in the show. Huell

Celebrating the California poppy.

was in great physical shape, and he and his guest would typically walk ahead of me (and my very heavy camera) at a strong and fast pace, sometimes leaving me in the dust. He'd glance at me from time to time to see where I was, and when he knew I was out of usable video range— or that I simply couldn't catch up—he'd stop and wait for me. I kept close track of his audio, and when I'd catch up with him I'd tell him where he was in the dialogue and ask him to pick it up from there. I'd reset the shot, he'd ask if I was ready, I'd get the camera up to speed, and off we'd go again on the walk-and-talk. For longer shots, I'd get far out in front of Huell and the interviewee so you could see them talking as they walked toward the camera, but I wouldn't record the audio. That way, the editor could seamlessly blend the dialogue and the video.

Speaking of which, although it was just Huell and I out in the field, we had essential help back at the studio—the distinctive look of *California's Gold* also came from the diligent and creative work of the editors who took my material and put it together to make a show. I always thought of them before I set up to shoot a scene, to give Huell and his editor more choices in assembling the show. I knew that Huell took copious notes before he went into the editing room, and although he walked in with a picture in his head of what he wanted, he gave certain editors leeway—especially the ones who had worked with him for some time and knew his style.

Another big plus that allowed me to concentrate during shoots was his great production staff. Phil Noyes was Huell's head producer for almost twenty years, and he and Harry Pallenberg, as well as a few other producers, took care of the logistics. They'd tell me where we were going to shoot, what weather conditions to expect, and what I should pack: boots and warm clothing for a winter show in the Sierra Nevada mountains, for instance, or light clothing and lots of water for a 115-degree shoot in Death Valley.

Two or three times a year, Huell and I went on ten-day road trips to shoot three shows in the same area of the state, or at locations that might not be very close but were easy to get to by highway. The producers did a great job of scheduling and handling the locations, interview contacts, and all the logistics that helped us get from one shoot to the next without a hitch.

Similarly, when we flew to our destination, Huell and I didn't have to concern ourselves with booking flights, car rentals, or hotels, because the producers took care of it. We'd get an itinerary before the travel days that told me what time to be at the airport, which airline we were flying, and when we'd be coming back. My only responsibility was to show up at the airport on time with my gear—the production staff expertly handled all the rest.

Phil, Harry, and the rest of the production team gave Huell and me the freedom to concentrate our efforts on the show, and I will be forever grateful for their hard work.

Don't look down! Luis on the Golden Gate Bridge.

THE PHYSICAL CHALLENGES

The camera I carried on most of the *California's Gold* shoots was heavy, unlike today's handheld digital cameras that are highly maneuverable and weigh only a few pounds. The twenty-four pounds of metal and glass that I carried on my shoulder were daunting, and I'd often have to hold the camera for hours at a time. I had to move my neck to the side to accommodate it and to be able to look into the viewfinder. Even today, years after retiring, I still have a few aches and pains in my neck and shoulder, but I just consider them reminders of all the work I did—work that, as you'll see in this section, could get pretty intense!

Technically, Huell owned the camera and equipment, but I was the one who took care of them. I never let them out of my sight, and I did everything but sleep with it all. When we flew, I didn't check the camera because I didn't trust the luggage handlers, so I carried it aboard the airplane, and it usually sat next to me. It was my tool, so if you liken it to a carpenter's saw, I always kept it sharp and ready to use.

The specific gear I carried on a shoot pretty much depended on what and where we were going. I'd get a call from one of Huell's producers (or sometimes the unit manager who worked for KCET), who would give me the basics about the shoot: what it was about, how many people we'd be interviewing at a time, where it was, how long we'd be there, the weather conditions I should expect, travel details, and so forth. I'd plan from there.

For a whitewater rafting shoot on the Kern River, for example, I got a special cover for the camera that protected it from the water. I shot a lot of the footage from another raft near Huell's, but some of the shots of him coming down the river in his raft were actually shot by me in the water—yes, while hoisting that heavy camera. I wore trunks in the frigid snowmelt water and held the camera up as I bobbed with the current to get the shots I needed to capture the action. Fortunately, I'm a strong swimmer, so I was able to get some great shots of the rapids while navigating the currents myself.

Proper lighting was usually pretty simple, as we shot most of the

Rafting the Kern River.

shows in the great outdoors. The sun was the main light source, as you would expect, and I'd set up Huell to take advantage of the direction it was coming from. I'd use the light on the camera only as necessary, perhaps if we were in the deep shade of a tree or building. If the shoot and interviews were taking place indoors, I'd pack soft and direct lights and perhaps reflectors. Sometimes, I had to pack the extra lighting and hike for some distance, but if I felt I needed it to get the job done, then I'd do it.

When we knew that Huell would be interviewing a few people at once, I'd bring more lavaliers, the small radio microphones we'd pin to their shirts. I'd stuff the battery pack that powered the mic into their back pocket, and we'd get clean, even sound. Huell was an expert with his handheld mic, speaking into it and moving it over to his guest, so his sound was always good.

In many situations, I'd have to walk backward so I could shoot Huell and a guest walking forward. The idea was to get a front shot of him talking with someone as they walked through a fascinating place—say, the redwoods, or a ghost town. You'd see them moving with the background changing, and I'd capture his reaction to something that he was looking at ahead of him—which meant behind me, so I couldn't even see what he was talking about. That was a curious feeling, often leaving me somewhat removed from the whole experience. Funny thing was, I was never scared or nervous, and I never thought about falling, I guess because I was so focused on the camera and the sound.

THE GREAT OUTDOORS

As all fans of the show know, Huell loved nature, especially Yosemite National Park. The show called "Yosemite Fire Fall" was a particularly trying one. The fire fall was a tradition going back to 1872, when the owner of a hotel at Glacier Point would put out the evening bonfire by kicking the embers off the cliff, inadvertently putting on a show for the

The Yosemite mule train getting ready to make the ascent.

people way down below in the valley. It became a tradition, a nightly (in season) spectacular fiery cascade that was occasionally halted for various reasons. Yosemite officials told us that they finally stopped the fire fall for good in 1968 because it was not a natural event, and of course it was terribly dangerous. I would have loved to have seen it.

For this episode, we were going up to Glacier Point. It was a heck of a way up, 3,200 feet above the valley floor. We started at dawn, riding sure-footed mules in a train that took almost three-quarters of the day to get to the top. Huell was riding ahead of me so I could shoot him experiencing the trip on the trail.

That ride up was tortuous and scary, as the edge of the trail often fell sharply hundreds of feet. I was able to aim the camera at Huell while simultaneously (and for no good reason) watching the drop-offs below. The mules had surely made the trip hundreds of times and knew what they were doing, but still....

I can't tell you how many times I stopped the mule train on that trail so I could get ahead of Huell and get a shot of him coming up the trail set against a background of Yosemite Valley below. He'd point to something, which was my cue to either point the camera to that same spot or get off the mule and shoot whatever he was pointing to so the editor would have the footage. Huell did a lot of that, and at that altitude, I was working very hard. We shot for only a few hours, and then had to turn around and come back down—and boy, was my butt sore. Unlike Huell, who was at ease in a saddle, I was an amateur at riding.

That episode included some old film footage of the bonfire setup on Glacier Point and the embers being pushed over, showcasing the spectacular fire fall. It also included some footage that Huell shot with his own camera—you can tell it's his because the pictures bounce around. He was kind enough to protect my reputation and let his viewers know that he took those shots. In the end, the show looked great, and it was definitely worth the hard work and that scary mule ride. You just can't beat the beauty of Yosemite.

I liked to wear shorts on most of the shoots, but we did some winter shoots in the Sierra that demanded that I wear warm clothing. My bulky jacket, heavy pants, and the freezing weather made shooting the show about the Southern Pacific Railroad snow sheds quite difficult—but, as it turned out, a lot of the footage that ended up in the show was archived footage of old steam engines in the snow sheds, so we didn't have to use all the video I shot. Thank goodness for that! I'm glad I thought of taking camera warmers for that shoot, because the temperature was constantly below freezing. I draped the small battery-powered electric blankets on the camera to keep the mechanisms warm, and I got some welcome heat for my hands, too.

Sometimes I carried so much gear that I felt like a Sierra pack mule. I guess that's why my last name is Fuerte—it means strong in Spanish. Usually, Huell carried only his microphone, which was fine by me, at least most of the time. Every now and then, though, the load became a challenge for me. One example was a 1999 shoot at Devil's Postpile near Mammoth, which tested us both. We were hiking on a long, steep mountain trail leading to Devil's Postpile, a spectacular volcanic rock formation, and I began falling behind. I was carrying a heavy load, including a bulky tripod I needed to give me a steady base to shoot the grandeur of the monument. I was beat and needed help. I called to Huell and asked if he would take the tripod. Thankfully, he did, and we got back on the trail. Losing that weight didn't exactly put a spring in my step, but man, I felt as if the weight of the world had been taken off my back.

After a short time, though, I saw Huell pawn the tripod off on someone who was hiking with us. When we got up to Devil's Postpile, I teased him about that, and he said the tripod got too heavy for him. You'd think that Mr. Marine would have volunteered to carry us all up the mountain!

One of the most arduous and trying shoots for me was the one we did on Santa Barbara Island. The challenge was that you can only go up or down on the island, and either way, it's not an easy journey. I had just turned fifty-three, and it was our fourth year together. We were hiking on a steep trail that pitched up sharply from the beach, and Huell, who was in his physical prime, was interviewing a park ranger who was pretty young and fit as well. The two men kept up a brisk pace on that slope, perhaps engaged in an unspoken competition to see who was the fittest and who'd be the first to need a break. Huell was absorbed in doing one of his long-form interviews, and the camera and I became invisible to him. I just couldn't keep up, and I finally shouted for them to stop for a bit because I was so tired. But I had a job to do, so I sucked it up and caught up with (and passed!) them at a good pace to set up for an approach shot. That sure showed them. Oh man, I was so beat by the end of the day—it felt as if I'd been run over by a truck.

Another physically challenging episode was when we went down deep into the Sixteen to One gold mine in the Sierra gold country. The mine has been worked since the mid-nineteenth century, but now it produces mostly what is called specimen gold. The shoot was a good example of the importance of getting location information from the producers. They warned me that it would likely be difficult and that I'd better prepare for unforeseen circumstances. So I did: I took along an extra set of batteries for the camera, a lot of extra lighting, and more batteries for the lights. Mines are dark, and I didn't know exactly what I'd need, so I thought it was better to bring everything. I was truly loaded down like a pack mule and pretty much prepared for anything, except perhaps a cave-in.

Even with the solid advance information, I didn't realize the full scope of that shoot and how trying it would be. I knew I'd be going deep into a mine—but the long descent thousands of feet into that mine shaft felt as if it would never end, like I was heading into a bottomless pit. I had to lie on my back on a trolley, the camera resting on my chest, while I rolled tape as I rocketed down the dark, narrow shaft. At times, the camera barely cleared the many rock outcroppings—I was terrified that each outcropping would rip the camera from my hands, sending it tumbling into the dark shaft and smashing it to bits. But when the trolley eased to a stop at the bottom, I still had the camera—and, as it turned out, some great images. That episode really put my skills and preparation—not to mention my nerves—to the test.

I knew I had charged the batteries the night before, and I'd also brought along spares. Yet I had a nagging thought that maybe I hadn't charged them enough; I worried that they might run out of juice, or, worse, that I'd have to tell Huell the batteries were gone and we had to stop shooting. The fear was irrational, I know, but when you're in a situation like that, with nowhere to go for fresh batteries, it happens. Fortunately, the batteries did what they were supposed to do, and the whole thing went very well. I think my Boy Scout "always be prepared" training definitely kicked in that day. We did so many shot setups in the Sixteen to One mine shoot that day that I felt like I was directing a movie. I sure hope all that effort comes across on camera.

Sometimes we went low, like into the mine, and sometimes we went high, like for the episode about the Giant Dipper, the 1924 wooden roller coaster at the Santa Cruz Beach Boardwalk. It's a thrilling ride that hits fifty-five miles per hour on the first big drop. Huell wanted to go on the ride, and, of course, I had to shoot him experiencing it.

To do it right, I figured it would involve two rides. The first would be just me alone, facing the rails in front to get what Huell's experience as a front-car passenger would look like. The second would be me sitting backward, shooting Huell as he went through all the dives and twists and turns of this great old roller coaster.

For the first ride, I got into the front car and was lashed down with a rope. I also ran the rope through the camera so it wouldn't fly out of my hands. The darn thing was a bulky twenty-four pounds, and I didn't want to hit a sharp curve and see it ripped out of my hands and launched into space. I was squashed in and couldn't put my eye to the viewfinder, so I just held the camera up, pushing it against the rope to steady it as best I could, pointed it straight ahead, and hoped for the best. I felt like a bull rider ready to bolt out of the chute. I said, "Okay, let's go," and off we went. The roller coaster did what big roller coasters do best: banging and jarring me around, but I kept the camera rolling all the way.

Afterward, Huell and I looked at the footage and were pleased that the camera stayed pointing forward and captured the thrill of the ride.

Then it was time to shoot Huell. He sat in the second car while I sat in the lead car, looking back at Huell so I could get his reactions. The camera and I were tied down again, I got the camera rolling, and off we went once more. I captured all the excitement of him holding on for dear life on that first scary drop, and then all his yelling and cheering as it whipped around sharp corners and tossed him from side to side. He was having a ball. We looked at the footage and liked it, so luckily, I didn't have to get strapped in and go on the darn thing a third time.

Another trying shoot was the one we did at Folsom Prison in 1995, which was difficult because it made both Huell and me very nervous. We were greeted outside the prison walls and had to strip down to our shorts before we were allowed inside—just in case either of us was trying to smuggle in drugs or weapons. They even checked my camera and equipment. We also had to sign a "hold harmless" agreement, so that if something happened to us the state wouldn't be held liable. *In case something happened to us?* No one had warned us about that. Phil? Harry?

Our guides said the reason we had to be checked out so thoroughly for contraband was that Folsom was one of the most violent prisons in the United States—a fact that was driven home as I shot Huell commenting on the bullet holes in the walls and ceiling near the prison entrance. As I was filming him walking into the prison, Huell noticed a painting inspired by Leonardo da Vinci's *The Last Supper*. A guide explained that the faces of the apostles in the painting were all murderers who were housed in the prison. That really didn't sit well with Huell, and it set an anxious tone for the both of us for the rest of the shoot.

Another rough element of that shoot was the situation we faced going out into the yard with the general population. We were told that if we wanted to do that, we would be on our own. Well, Huell insisted on shooting there, so I dutifully followed him with the camera. I tell you, I had one eye in the viewfinder and the other on whoever was around me and how they were moving. I didn't want to be taken hostage or shanked for no good reason. That was a tense shoot that I would probably would refuse to do again, if asked.

There were a lot more situations that pushed me in new ways, such as the show at Amboy Crater, shot in 115-degree heat. I almost passed out on the steep climb up and had to stop production to collect myself.

Another was the Bristlecone Pines shoot, when we were at 9,000 feet in the White Mountains. I did a lot of taxing setups on that shoot and got a severe altitude headache for my efforts. Come to think of it, more than just the headache, this shoot stands out to me as the first time Huell really got carried away with his "amazing" descriptions of everything in sight. There wasn't a single ancient pine tree that didn't get the Huell gushing treatment. He was definitely in his element, and that made me very happy—despite the throbbing pain in my head.

BLOOPERS, BLUNDERS, & THINGS GONE WRONG

One day, we went to the old Camp Lockett in Campo, down toward San Diego, to shoot a reunion of World War II veterans who were members of the last horse-mounted cavalry in the United States. The attendees also included the last veterans of the Buffalo Soldiers, the all-black military horse unit that had fought heroically in many American battles. They were a fun group, telling Huell great stories about their adventures at Camp Lockett as young men training to ride their steeds into battle. A few of the veterans even got up into saddles after fifty years and showed Huell how they rode their horses military-style.

At the end of the shoot, Huell asked me, "Louie, how do you think we should finish the show?"

I looked around and said, "Well, the sun is right, it's getting late in the day, and the light is perfect. We're in a nice valley, and it's beautiful. Why don't you and the guys ride your horses off into the sunset? That'll be the closing shot, and we'll roll credits over that."

Huell liked the idea, so I set the camera in the field to get the sunset shot and lined up Huell and the soldiers on their mounts. I rolled the

One of many physically demanding shoots in the Sierra.

Huell and a horse in happier times.

camera, got speed, and shouted, "All right, action!" and they took off, horses charging, riding into the sunset, just like in the movies. Except that Huell fell off his horse.

As he got up and dusted himself off, I could see that he hadn't suffered any real damage, so I pulled a Cecil B. DeMille on him and shouted, "Huell, you ruined my shot! How could you fall off the horse and ruin my shot?"

It turned out that the saddle hadn't been cinched tightly, so it slipped and rotated on the horse, and off Huell went. I tried, but I could not convince him to get back on the horse and do a second take, even though we still had that west light streaming in low and I could get the great film shot I'd envisioned. But I did manage to finish the show with a gorgeous shot of the landscape at sunset. It really would have been so much nicer with Huell astride his horse, charging into battle.

I drove the Explorer home and kept hearing, "Oh, my knee! Oh, my leg, it hurts!" He often talked about his time in the Marines, so I finally teased him back by saying, "I thought you were a Marine. What were you, in supply?" My good-natured chiding hit home, and he cut down on the complaints—but he still whimpered all the way back to the studio.

California's Gold says it all. The title of the show tells you that what you're about to see was shot in the Golden State, right? Not necessarily—Huell managed to pull off a big, big stretch to get us on a steamboat that sails the Mississippi River. That's right—more than two thousand miles from California.

The show was about the *Delta Queen*, a sternwheel riverboat that had been built in California in the 1920s along with its twin, the *Delta King*. In 1946 it was moved east via the Panama Canal to get restored in Pittsburgh and then ply the Mississippi for decades as a

Huell interviewing the captain of the *Delta Queen*.

historic landmark. The boat was a living part of old California, plus it was a National Historic Landmark, and that was reason enough for Huell to set us off on a journey to Louisiana.

We spent four days on that boat learning (and shooting) everything about it, from the time it sailed on the Sacramento River to the present day. I shot Huell with an older gentleman who, back in his twenties in the 1930s, was an engineer on the ship. He was delighted to see that the engine room hadn't changed from back in his day. I shot pretty much every nook and cranny in that engine room, and it felt good to be in that noisy hull, with all that polished steel whirling in steady circles, transforming energy into the power that turned the rear paddle wheel. It took me back to the days I served on a Navy destroyer, although it wasn't propelled by a paddle wheel. I'm not that old!

This was the first time I'd been in the South, and I was lucky to get to experience Southern hospitality at its finest. Huell was radiantly in his element. As the days went by, his accent got heavier and heavier, and it was great to see him relaxed and feeling at home with folks who spoke his tongue.

Huell absolutely fell in love with the *Delta Queen*. It represented a connection with California's olden days that he so much wanted to be a part of, plus it had a new life in the South. He wanted to reclaim it and take it back to California, get it back to work on the Sacramento River where he thought it belonged. I wish he could have; in 2008, long after we shot this episode of *California's Gold*, the boat was permanently taken out of service for financial reasons and turned into a hotel.

I met a lot of fascinating people that day, and I'm still in touch with a few of them. I still think it was a bit suspect to go to Louisiana for *California's Gold*, but I sure am glad Huell made that stretch.

In all the years of videotaping hundreds of programs with Huell, I fell only once, while I was walking backward with my camera. It happened during a shoot for a program called "Terra Cotta." We were up north in a town called Lincoln at the Gladding McBean foundry, which makes terra-cotta statues and fancy, one-of-a-kind clay architectural pieces. Huell was doing one of his walking interviews that he favored, and I was walking backward (as I always did) to get the shot. The place was about as dark as the sky slipping into night. I'd turned on the sun-gun light mounted on the camera, but I was barely getting enough light on them to make the picture usable.

I always looked back to see where I was going, but I couldn't make out anything because the camera's light blinded me to the dark behind me. Huell was about to end the interview when my foot caught on a small step and I fell backward on my butt. The camera rolled on, shooting a streak of video. Huell hurried over to see if I was okay, worried that I'd been hurt. I got up, embarrassed, and said, "Yeah, yeah, I'm fine,

Strapping in before takeoff with the Blue Angels.

Huell. Now let's pick it up so I can make a cut."

The camera never hit the ground. That's what my body was for.

We did a couple of shows in El Centro, a town deep in the Colorado Desert in the southeast corner of California. One revolved around shooting the Blue Angels—the famous Navy and Marine aerobatic team that was based there. The guys put Huell in a spiffy-looking G-suit and took him to one of their hot, fast F/A-18 Hornets to be the man riding in the back seat, like Goose in the movie *Top Gun*. They strapped him in, and the pilot took that baby straight up, pulling some big Gs. Then he flew a few loops and made some sharp turns, racing around the sky in a howl of jet noise before he landed.

Huell climbed out of the jet and promptly threw up. I didn't get it on tape, but at least he had the good manners to wait until he got back on the ground.

For the other El Centro shoot, we started out at dawn for a good long drive to do a *Visiting with Huell Howser* show about life there. When we got to El Centro, however, the people we were supposed to interview didn't show up.

We just sat there in the car with the air conditioner blowing, out in the middle of the hot, dry desert some two hundred miles from home. Things looked bleak. Huell asked if I had any ideas for how to salvage the situation, to at least get something on tape. The best thing I could think of was to go to a cool bar and discuss the situation; maybe we could salvage the drive and come up with an idea. All we needed was some creativity—which is what bars are for, right?

He thought that sounded reasonable, so we drove around until we found a bar. It sure didn't look like much, but we sat down with a couple of beers and talked about the situation. After a while, Huell looked around, taking in the place, the bartender, and the patrons, and then he looked at me, eyebrows raised. His wheels were turning, and I caught on pretty quick.

He said, "What do you think, Louie?"

I looked around and said, "Why not? Let's talk to the bartender. They always have stories and know what's going on."

So Huell talked to the bartender, who gave him some input on who was interesting around there to talk to, and what might be worth shooting. We filmed a short segment in the bar, and on the bartender's advice, headed to the local newspaper. Somehow, Huell worked his magic to stretch and stretch and stretch the little information we had—and we got a show! To this day, I don't really remember what it was about, but it was fun and it worked.

Another bust of an outing happened on the shoot for the show that Huell called "Blossom Trails." He'd received a letter raving about the magnificent beauty of the flowering fruit trees in Reedley, a small farm town in Fresno County. It went on to say that the blooms wouldn't last forever, and if we didn't take immediate advantage of this opportunity, we'd lose the show of a lifetime—or something to that effect.

Huell was a huge flower lover and couldn't resist the sales pitch, so up we went on what we both thought would be an easy, one-day shoot, as the drive over the Grapevine and into the San Joaquin Valley was only a few hours from the studio.

We pulled off the 99 at the Reedley exit and began looking for the great groves of trees loaded with those luscious flowers. We drove miles in and all around Reedley searching for the big blooms. We found flowers all right, but they weren't the ones described so glowingly in the letter. We spotted a few flowers here and there on the trees, but hardly enough to make a show. Apparently our hot tip was old information, and we'd probably missed the big bloom by a few weeks. But Huell didn't want to let the drive go to waste. He said, "We're here, Louie, let's try to make something of it!" Once again, Huell worked his unique gift for making a silk purse out of a sow's ear. He took the wheel of the Explorer and drove us back into Reedley, where after a bit of exploration, he found the Mennonite Quilt Center, introduced us to an Armenian delicacy called *keyma* at Uncle Harry's Classic Meals, and encountered the world's longest-running pinochle game at the Camden Café. The show called "Blossom Trails" turned out nothing like we'd originally planned, but there were a few blossoms—and viewers discovered that Reedley was a whole lot more interesting than it seemed upon first glance.

THEMED SHOWS
&
OPPORTUNITY SHOOTS

Huell was big on themed shows and opportunity shoots. The themed shows were *California's Gold* programs that featured segments with a common thread but not directly related to one another—nor were they likely shot on the same day. There were theme shows on just about anything you can imagine, from "Trees" to "Flying Fish" to "Neat Houses," and we'd shoot all over the state to make them.

The opportunity shoots often wound up in theme shows, and they usually happened by chance. Typically, Huell and I would be driving to or from a location shoot when one of us would spot something interesting. We'd stop the car, Huell would hunt for someone to talk to, and if it worked out, we'd shoot something there spontaneously.

One of the opportunity shoots that I'll never forget was the field of marigolds we drove by in the Las Posas Valley—we were in the Camarillo area on the way to another shoot and just happened to come upon miles of marigolds, a rolling sea of gold and orange. To quote Huell, it was amaaazing. We got out of the car at the side of the road and Huell searched for someone to talk to about this spectacular sight. He finally located a couple of brothers who were growing the flowers, and he interviewed them amid the marigolds in the fields.

What made this shoot memorable was Huell's reaction to the brothers' answer to his question about where the flowers were destined. He was, of course, expecting to hear that they were going to flower shops. But they said that all those gorgeous orange petals were destined to become chicken feed, because the marigolds helped make the egg yolks a richer color.

Huell looked as shocked as if he'd just stuck his finger in a light socket. I thought he was going to fall over! Then, when the delightful surprise about coloring eggs hit his funny bone, he broke out in that huge Huell grin.

"Chicken feed? To color *chicken feed?!*" he exclaimed in that marvelous Tennessee accent. His reaction really is hilarious.

Huell's long-term approach to *California's Gold* was one of the things that made the show so successful. He knew that if he found and shot enough varied and interesting segments, over time they'd fit with other segments he had in the can or was going to shoot, and he'd have a show. If he already had a couple of segments that seemed related, he'd take me out and we'd shoot another one that would fit in, and then we'd have a show. I never saw the bank of all the segments that I shot, but it must have been impressive.

The themed show "Wind" comprised the usual three segments. We visited the Warner Brothers Burbank lot to see a studio wind machine in action, the historic Caltech wind tunnel, and Point Reyes, which was, according to Huell, typically the windiest place in California. I'm guessing that Huell saw the Caltech and Burbank shoots as local and easy to shoot, and then waited for an opportunity to go to Point Reyes when we were up north for something else.

One of my favorite themed shows (and one of Huell's favorites as well) was called "Big Things in the Desert." I'll just say that "Big" was an understatement. I shot Huell by the sky-high windmills at a wind farm off the 10 Freeway near Palm Springs: Huell with the massive dump

That's an amaaazingly big truck!

trucks that hauled 190 tons of boron at a time out of a vast pit mine dug deep into the desert floor; and Huell standing on the two hundred-foot-wide cradle of an antenna at Goldstone that searched deep space. Each segment took a whole day to shoot, but it was so much fun that Huell didn't mind at all.

These were big toys for big boys: huge wheels, massive hunks of metal, and gigantic whirling blades. What more could a man ask for? The immense size of the trucks especially floored Huell. I heard "Oh, my gosh!" again and again as he approached one of those monsters and crawled around it. The colossal antennas at Goldstone also produced an abundance of "Louie, look at this!" and "Oh, my gosh, this is *amaaazing!*"

Over the years, I shot countless themed show segments on so many subjects at so many different locations that it's hard to remember them all. But plenty still seem like it was yesterday. One favorite memory is

Luis in the fog at Morro Rock.

when Huell and I were driving past a big cactus farm in bloom in the Salinas Valley. It caught his eye and we pulled over. I told him that Mexican people called that cactus *nopales* and they enjoyed eating it. He said he'd been thinking of doing a show called "Bits and Pieces," and he thought this would be perfect for it. So he went out among the cactus and talked with some farmworkers in the fields. I got the equipment out of the car and shot Huell interacting with the harvest workers. The cactus segment fit perfectly in the "Bits and Pieces" show, and it happened entirely by accident.

Many times we'd purposely go out to shoot things at their optimum time, like the wildflower fields in the spring at peak bloom. Or Huell would learn of an annual parade somewhere and we'd go out and shoot it. If Huell saw an opportunity to shoot something that was timely and interesting, we'd jump into the car and go.

Most of those segments went hand in hand with other segments in a themed show, but sometimes, his idea of what the segments had in common hung by a thin thread. One of the theme shows that tested the bounds of commonality was "California's Tallest, Prettiest, and Rockiest"—I'm not sure what "tallest" had to do with "rockiest," and I just thought of it as the superlative show. We shot it all over California, usually when we were en route to or from a shoot for another episode.

For the "Tallest" portion, we traveled to the Eureka area, where I shot a grove of redwoods. I was awestruck at the majesty of those giants.

The "Prettiest" segment ended up being about the poppy preserve near Lancaster. It had been a great rain year when we visited, so the poppies were particularly prolific and glorious. We were just winging it, shooting the flowers with Huell walking among them and talking to whomever he found. I don't know if Huell had the "-est" show in mind that day, but he knew he could use the footage somewhere, and besides, he adored poppies and wanted to be among them.

The third segment of the superlative show was about Morro Rock, with Huell proclaiming that it was the "Rockiest." That was a messy shoot. Countless birds use that big hunk of rock as their outdoor rest-room—big time—and I had a heck of time keeping my footing and holding the heavy camera as I slipped and slid on the stuff. But I managed without falling, and that eventually became the final segment of "California's Tallest, Prettiest, and Rockiest."

Those opportunity shoots were essential to the success of *California's Gold*, and the only reason they worked is because Huell was so bold and fearless in his quest to get something great on camera. He was always watching for an opportunity, and I never knew when he'd suddenly stop the car, walk up to anyone and everyone on public or private property, interrupt whatever they were doing, and charm them into letting us interview them and shoot the location. They just couldn't resist Huell's big smile and Southern warmth, and in no time flat, we'd have a great segment.

THE CALIFORNIA MISSIONS

It was Huell who came up with the idea to do a series about the California missions. We were down in Loreto, Baja California, doing a shoot for another program that wasn't part of *California's Gold*. Our guide took us sightseeing and showed us an old Spanish mission nearby. He explained how the Spanish padres started building missions in Baja first and then worked their way north. Huell was interested and said in passing that we should shoot the California missions. That was the last I heard of it for some time, until one day in 1997 when he announced, "Guess what, Louie? We're doing the missions—all twenty-one of the ones in California!"

I said, "You gotta be kidding me, Huell."

He said, "Nope, we're going to do the missions—*all* of them."

The cost of the mission series was outside of the usual budget that Huell had for *California's Gold*, so he got a sponsor for those shows and announced to the world that we were going to do a series of shows about the missions, and that's exactly what we did.

In retrospect, I don't think he quite understood at first what a great undertaking the task of shooting all the missions on such a short schedule would be. There's a heck of a lot of them, and California is a big state. Huell figured that we could shoot two to three a day, starting early for the first shoot, breaking down the gear and driving to the next one at about midday, where we'd set up, shoot, and break down, and then hustle to the next mission, where we'd repeat the process before dark. I thought it would be extremely challenging, just from the logistics end, without even taking into account the scouting and shooting of each mission. The show's producers did a great job of providing materials, photos, and interviews, so we weren't flying completely blind. But both the schedule and the hundreds of miles we had to cover made me uneasy.

Our schedule of seven to eight shooting days was ambitious, but we committed ourselves to it. We added travel days and overnight stays for the far-flung missions and came up with a schedule we could hang our hats on. We didn't shoot the missions one after the other, day after day: it actually took about three weeks to visit them all. In between we

Mission San Luis Rey de Francia.

had other *California's Gold* shoots to do, so we covered the missions here and there until we had all twenty-one in the can.

We began with the first and southernmost mission built in California, San Diego de Alcalá, just off the 8 Freeway in San Diego. That morning, Huell was as excited as a kid on Christmas morning. Our host was a docent who cheerfully took us on a tour, dropping lots of facts on the equally cheerful Huell. We got good material and finished in a quick two to three hours. We were on schedule and we were happy, so we wrapped up and hit the road.

At noon, we arrived at Mission San Luis Rey de Francia, thirty-nine miles from San Diego. Our guide, a brother who lived at the mission, took Huell on a walking tour of the grounds, and the two eventually found themselves in front of a huge tree. The brother told Huell that the tree, planted in 1830, was the first pepper tree planted in California and was, in fact, the mother of all California pepper trees.

Huell was taken aback. He put his hand on the brother's shoulder and said, somewhat apologetically, "Not that I'm doubting you, but how do you know it's the oldest pepper tree in California?"

The priest eyed Huell directly, a scolding look on his face, and said, "What a question."

That didn't settle well with Huell, who was fixed on this quest for truth. He asked, "But how do you *know* this tree goes back to 1830?"

The brother's stern look dissolved and he broke out in laughter, pointing to the nearby lawn sign. He said, "Haven't you read that sign over there?" Huell realized he'd gotten all the answers he was going to get about the tree, and the rest would have to be taken on faith.

He laughed heartily with our guide, and off we went to Mission San Juan Capistrano, famed for the swallows that return year after year to nest in its eaves and crannies, although nowadays there are few swallows left. The mission is a very active church, and Huell spent most of the show talking with people and covering the events that the parish children put on just for him.

We'd done it—we shot the first three missions in one day on schedule, and everything went well.

The next time out, two of the three missions were pretty close to each other: Mission San Gabriel in the San Gabriel Valley and Mission San Fernando in, well, the San Fernando Valley. The third was Mission Buenaventura up the coast in Ventura, which meant a pretty good drive north on the 101.

We were at Mission San Gabriel at eight in the morning. The church's Moorish-style architecture is a copy of a church in Spain, and it's impressive to see up close. The morning was gray and overcast, and the colors were muted so the shots came out flat. But Huell got to ring his first mission bell, which made his day.

We got to Mission San Fernando by noon. It's off a busy street, which throws off plenty of traffic noise that you hear in the show—I tried, but I just couldn't get away from it. Governor Pico lived at the mission in its early, quieter days, and it has the distinction of being the largest adobe building in California. Huell went through it pretty fast, as we were anxious to get on the road for the long ride to Mission San Buenaventura, the last mission built by Junipero Serra.

It was a highlight because of the excavation next door of the old foundation and Native American sites. Huell *loved* to get in on that kind of stuff. At the end of the day, we had six missions under our belt in just two shooting days. We were pleased and optimistic about the upcoming ones.

The next shoot day started at Mission Santa Barbara, in the heights above the city. We arrived just after the sun came up, as the other two missions for the day were some distance away. A gregarious brother wearing a robe of the early era met us out front. The mission is called the Queen of the Missions, and indeed it is gorgeous. Huell loved it and insisted that I capture all of its beauty, so we took our time exploring and shooting it. This, of course, put us behind schedule. So we had to really hustle to the next location, Mission Santa Inés.

Mission Santa Inés.

As we pulled into the mission's parking lot, we saw a plume of smoke shooting up from behind it. Huell got out and helped put out the small fire that was working its way through wood chips on the ground. I taped his good deed, but it put us even more behind schedule. Because we were so late, Huell decided that we'd only shoot outside, as the church was located in such a lovely setting. It was a shame that we didn't have the time to shoot inside, and we both felt badly about it.

We hurried off and arrived quite late at Mission La Purisima Concepción. Thankfully, our hosts were understanding and patient. The striking, architecturally significant mission is inside a state historical park, and costumed actors/docents reenact life during its prime. We shot inside first to make sure we'd have visuals this time, and Huell loved the pastoral setting so much that we spent the remainder of the day in a field full of farm animals. He asked me to shoot an actor dressed in a traditional Native American costume feeding carrots to a big ox.

And when I say big ox, I mean a *really* big ox. It had been rubbing its head up and down on the actor's body, trying, I suppose, to urge him to speed up the snacks. Suddenly, it lunged and almost crushed him. He wasn't hurt, but it was intense to see an ox's way of telling you it wants more carrots—now.

Many more animals in the pasture were looking for handouts, including a rather large horse behind Huell. While he was interviewing people about their roles, he kept glancing over his shoulder at the horse. I could hear the concern in his voice—he was obviously worried that it was going to give him a dose of what the ox had given the actor. Mostly, though, Huell loved the animals, and even though we'd made sure to shoot inside the mission, the edited show was mostly about the animals. Check it out and you'll see.

Our fourth day of mission shoots took us up the coast to the missions San Luis Obispo, San Miguel, and San Antonio de Padua. The

Mission San Miguel.

first was Mission San Luis Obispo de Tolosa, which we'd visited before for one of the first *California's Gold* shows. Huell's guide was an outgoing history professor from Cal Poly San Luis Obispo who regaled Huell with engaging stories. Although we shot inside the church, Huell edited the program so that only the outside was shown.

We then drove the thirty-six miles to Mission San Miguel, far off the beaten path halfway between Los Angeles and San Francisco. Built as a quadrangle in 1797, the old mission, one of only a few that are National Historic Landmarks, had not yet been restored. (It has since enjoyed a significant restoration that is nearing completion.) The docent told Huell that it looked as it did in 1820, a fact that captivated him. He was thrilled about its originality and in awe of its original structures and frescoes. He kept asking exuberantly, "This is the original color? The original paint?"

The third mission on that shoot, San Antonio de Padua, is in an undeveloped, pastoral part of the Fort Hunter Ligett Military Reservation, so our producers had gotten us permission to shoot there. Huell got caught up in the wonder of it all, and how its isolation helps visitors get a sense of what early mission life would have been like. At times, like when he touched the old adobe walls, Huell's joy and awe seemed to almost overwhelm him.

Twelve missions down, nine to go.

The next batch were Nuestra Señora de la Soledad and San Carlos Borromeo del río Carmelo, and we tacked that shoot day onto the same road trip that took us to the three previous Central California missions. Like San Miguel, Mission Soledad is isolated. The mission had to be completely reconstructed, as over a century and a half it had decayed; its roof tiles had been removed and rain and wind had eroded the structure into piles of adobe soil. There was a feeling of melancholy surrounding the place, and Huell was unusually quiet, not the high-energy guy he'd been the day before.

Seventy-four miles later, we arrived at the mission known simply as

Carmel Mission. We shot both the inside and outside, and I got some good shots of the great Moorish tower that reflects Spain's Arabic history, as well as Father Serra's burial site, which really affected Huell.

We shot Mission San Juan Bautista on a different day, so we could spend more time there. This mission particularly fascinated Huell, and he had a lot of fun with it. The seemingly haphazard construction—a combination of old Spanish and nineteenth-century New England clapboard—doesn't look like any of the other missions. Our guide explained that the original church had been damaged heavily in an earthquake along the nearby San Andreas fault and was rebuilt by New Englanders who had settled the area. They rebuilt the damaged parts in the style they were familiar with, and the result is a rather goofy hodgepodge. On the serious side, Huell toured the graveyard and experienced deep sorrow about the four thousand Native Americans who are buried there. He told viewers how it had helped him understand the devastating toll that the missions and colonization had taken on California's native population.

Next was Mission Santa Cruz, which Huell learned is nicknamed the Hard-Luck Mission. It was utterly destroyed in the epic 1857 Fort Tejon earthquake on the San Andreas fault, and the building that Huell and I surveyed was a replica of the original. Huell was clearly disappointed that there was nothing left of the original building to show his viewers. We discussed our options with our host; perhaps we could follow him as he led Huell through the grounds and the replica mission. Or, our guide said, maybe we could shoot the small adobe buildings nearby that had housed Native American neophytes, the new converts to Christianity.

Not surprisingly, this piqued Huell's interest. The little adobes had withstood the earthquake that had taken down the mission, and Huell found their history to be particularly meaningful. He decided to build most of the show around them, which is why there was so little about the mission itself in the final show.

The shoot at Mission Santa Clara de Asís was very difficult for Huell. Located on the campus of Santa Clara University, it has been ruined and rebuilt six times. He was terribly disappointed and struggled to find a way to make a show around a mission that had no present sense of history. But he'd pledged to shoot all the missions. And so, being the trouper that he was, he created a show on the fly, and I followed him around and shot it.

Next was Mission San José, only seventeen miles away. Huell was energized again, because at least some of the original mission had survived. The original bells, for instance, were in the tower, remnants of the first tower, which had been destroyed (along with the rest of the mission) by an earthquake in 1868; the current mission is an exact replica of the original. It was here that Huell finally understood that rebuilding these relics of California's history was a necessity, given the state's succeptibility to damaging earthquakes. He was impressed with the pre-earthquake art that had survived, along with the hammered, copper baptismal font that had been used to baptize more than 6,500 Native Americans. Huell was liberal with his declarations of "Gee!" and "Oh, wow!" and he ended our visit by proclaiming, "This is the most *amaaazing* story of all the missions!" Now that was saying something.

Three final missions—San Francisco de Asís, San Rafael Arcángel, and San Francisco Solana—marked the end of our mission-shooting journey, and we covered them all on the same day. That morning, Huell was as lighthearted as I had ever seen him. He was positively radiant! I was happy, too, and we laughed and chattered like little kids on the last day of school. This was going to be a fun day.

When we arrived at Mission San Francisco de Asís, widely known as Mission Dolores, Huell set the mood and significance of the day by telling viewers that it was "the last day of our mission quest." We began shooting the curiously small and skinny main mission building, which our guide said was the most original, intact, and narrowest of all the missions, as well as the oldest structure in San Francisco. Huell went on and on (as only he could) about how this mission was the best preserved one we'd seen. He loved everything he heard from our guide, and he was amazed that the narrow construction was the reason it had withstood even the violent 1989 Loma Prieta earthquake.

Nothing short of another big shaker was going to spoil his day. We finished shooting and headed north to San Rafael and Mission San Rafael Arcángel. The mission's curator told Huell right off the bat that not only was it completely new, it didn't look anything like the original. Known as "the most obliterated" of the missions, it nonetheless had a very colorful history, including serving as a fort for Gen. John Fremont during the battle to make California a part of the United States. Also, Kit Carson had ridden out from the fort. Huell had plenty to learn and share with his viewers.

The last mission of the day (and the series) was San Francisco Solano. Huell was thrilled to learn that it was the last mission built before Mexico's 1834 secularization of the mission system, and it held the only post-mission-era chapel, which was built in 1842. He didn't care when he learned that it was a complete replica. I knew what he was thinking: "It's a replica, so what? Lots of the missions are replicas. I'm okay with that. This is the last one. Let's shoot, Louie!"

At the tail end of that shoot, Huell looked right into the camera and, with great relief and satisfaction, said, "We're packing up and going home. We have completed our quest to visit all twenty-one wonderful and beautiful missions."

I was happy, too, with our achievement, and I felt like we'd just stumbled onto the beach after swimming the Catalina Channel. It was a big, big job, and we were both proud of the work we'd done.

I have to mention something funny that Huell said around the eighteenth or nineteenth mission. He was starting to get overwhelmed by the enormity of the task of doing great episodes on every single mission in California, especially considering our tight schedule and budget. We were outside a mission, just looking at it and talking about what to shoot, when he said, "Louie, I'm getting over-missioned. If we keep going, I may just become a Catholic."

I said, "Well, if you do that, Huell, you'll have to go to confession and confess all your sins to a priest."

He said, "*All* of them?"

"Every one."

Huell screwed up his face and said, "Well, Louie, I might just have to think about that."

After shooting the last mission, we stowed the gear in the Explorer and visited a bar. He raised his glass and said, "We did it. We did it, Louie, all twenty-one." I'm not sure, but we may have saluted each and every mission with a drink that night—all I know is that I didn't get around to cleaning the gear.

The shows about the missions were some of the most beautiful Huell and I ever did, and they were certainly among the most fascinating and important. The old churches, the stories of the padres, the building and rebuilding and rebuilding again, the earthquakes, the eventual devastation of the native peoples—all this brought out deep feelings in Huell, and they enriched his love of California and its history.

SHOOTS
I'LL ALWAYS REMEMBER

Of the hundreds of *California's Gold* shoots Huell and I did together, my favorite and the most fun was the Golden Gate Bridge shoot. That show seems to be a favorite of his fans, too. It was one of the most technically challenging shows I ever shot, as well as one of the most creative, because it gave me the opportunity to shoot it as if we were doing a film.

The Golden Gate Bridge is a meaningful part of California, and I think many people view the promise of California in that bridge. It's also one of most beautiful structures on earth—just thinking of it fills me with emotion. I knew I had to shoot it so the majesty of its impressive structure would be revealed. Thankfully, the day was beautiful and clear, without the fog that usually shrouds San Francisco. With only a few clouds off in the distance, it made for a picturesque sight.

I thought we were booked for one helicopter, but as it turned out, we had two at our disposal. Imagine that—two helicopters, just for us! We decided to shoot Huell and his guest taking off toward the bridge in one while I shot Huell doing the interview in the other. Both of us circled back to land, and then I got into Huell's helicopter to capture a second take of his interview against the beautiful Bay Area scenery.

That took a lot of time and trouble, but I couldn't pass up the chance to create an episode with multiple perspectives, thanks to the two helicopters—it made a one-camera show look like a multi-camera show. The pilots were happy to do what I asked, and I will always be grateful to them for giving me the opportunity to be creative.

Of all the footage we shot that day, I think what impressed me the most was flying under the bridge. What a great shooting perspective, and what a thrill; I was like a kid in a candy store. With so many stunning shots, we easily could have edited the interview into a sixty-minute show. I don't think the bridge has ever been covered so well in a one-camera shoot, and I'm pleased to say I was the one behind the camera. I still get a lot of comments from other camera operators asking how I did it, and their praise means a lot to me.

After the flights, we drove back onto the bridge and got into an elevator that took us near the top. We made our way to the upper platform and stepped out into the brisk bay wind. To the south lay beautiful San Francisco, its buildings covering the undulating hills. The bay was hundreds of feet below us, and I began to feel—with a thrill and twinge of fear—how high up we were. I mean, this is the top of the Golden Gate Bridge we're talking about. And though climbing up with all of my camera gear was tricky, it was a once-in-a-lifetime filming opportunity.

Huell had a lot of fun on that trip. Ever the one to capture the human experience, he interviewed men who were replacing the original rivets, and he even spoke with the old-timers who had pounded in those red-hot rivets back when the bridge was built in the 1930s. He also talked to the painters who spend their lives keeping the bridge that striking golden-orange color. They told Huell that some painters don't last through their first day because of the cold winds and frightening height. After being up on the top of that bridge, I really do understand why.

All the preparation and grunt work that went into the shoot was worth it. The other day, I was watching the Golden Gate Bridge show

Good thing Louie wasn't afraid of heights!

with my wife, Gloria. She asked me how I got from my helicopter (from which I was shooting Huell and his pilot) into the other helicopter with Huell. I told her I had jumped over. She almost believed me, so I told her the truth. But a successful leap through the whirling blades sure would have made a great story.

Personally, I think this shoot was the most beautiful show we ever did. I'm really proud of it—both how it looked and the way it was shot. People tell me all the time that the Golden Gate Bridge show is their favorite *California's Gold* episode. But I can't take all the credit. The truth is, that remarkable bridge told me just how to shoot it so that I could show it off at its best.

Another favorite show I did with Huell is a *Visiting with Huell Howser* shoot about the ornate vaudeville and movie theaters built in the 1920s and '30s that line Broadway in downtown Los Angeles. I just love the look of that show, but it was memorable for other reasons as well. Huell said he wanted to interview this guy on the sidewalk, and if you're familiar with that stretch of Broadway, you know just how crowded the sidewalk can be on a shopping Saturday.

"It'll be just me and the person I'm interviewing, and we'll walk for half a block and that's it. Get the flavor of the street," he said. Half a block soon turned into three blocks. Whenever Huell got inspired, he lost track of time—and sometimes, even me.

I like to shoot people from the front, or sometimes from the side, depending on the look I'm going for. I decided to walk backward all the way, shooting Huell and his guest, constantly looking back to see what I was going to run into while keeping the camera steady. The thick crowds parted as we journeyed down the street, with Huell going full tilt on the interview, seemingly oblivious to me.

Getting ready to walk backward through downtown LA.

At one point, I lost my perspective and I didn't know where I was on the sidewalk. I slowed my walk and let them catch up with me, then did a 360-degree turn around them as they continued their walk and talk. Halfway through the circle, I nearly collided with a mailbox, but I got my bearings and repositioned myself in front of them, and Huell got the interview in one long take.

Other cameramen who saw that single-shot interview commented about the complete circle I made around Huell, saying, "I loved that 360 that you did!" and "That was a nice creative touch." I had to be honest, so I told them I did that 360 to save the camera (and me!) from what could have been a nasty tumble. I still think the shot is one of my best, and I'm proud of the sixteen uncut minutes we captured in that scene.

Another memorable show was one we shot on the B-2 stealth bomber up in Palmdale. I love machinery and technical stuff and, man, I was so happy that Huell had chosen to do the show on the bomber. I was in heaven. I got to sit at the controls and pretend that I was flying this big, beautiful baby—it sure felt good. Of course, every bit of footage I shot had to be closely examined by the government so I wouldn't give away any military secrets. It all looked pretty complicated—I wouldn't have even known what I was giving away.

Huell was as excited as I had ever seen him when we were shooting that impressive airplane. He just may have set the *California's Gold* record for the number of "gollys" and "gee whizzes" he uttered—maybe even more than during the "Big Things in the Desert" show.

THE TRIP TO TBILISI

In April of 1993, Huell and I traveled to Europe for a special program he was really excited to shoot. It didn't turn out as he had planned, and ended with us coming home with plenty of footage but nothing that captured our original vision for the show. Yet this shoot-gone-bad may have been the most important event that we ever recorded on tape.

Our destination was Tbilisi, the capital of Georgia, a former state of the Soviet Union. The plan was to shoot the first private airlift of much-needed medications to a hospital in the city, with Huell accompanying the humanitarian team to document the mission. Huell saw it as an opportunity to show his viewers that there were good people in the world helping those in need. The show was supposed to be positive and uplifting. What we witnessed was the aftermath of the dissolution of the Soviet Union and the terrible toll it had taken on the common people.

We were scheduled to leave in the early morning on a plane that was destined to land in Dallas with a stopover in Florida, but things didn't go well from the beginning. As we taxied toward the runway, the plane's wing hit a hangar and the wing-tip light got smashed. Though it was ultimately repaired, the process wound up delaying every other leg of our trip. That accident was an omen for what was to come.

Once in the air, Huell sat down to interview Harry Thomason, the well-known co-producer of the long-running television series *Designing Women*. Harry, a good friend and admirer of Huell's work, was part of the humanitarian effort in Tbilisi and the man responsible for helping us do a story about the mercy flight. Harry and two of his boyhood friends from Arkansas, Hayden McElroy and Jim Blair, had volunteered to pay for the flights in and out of Georgia, and they'd arranged for the airplane and crew to fly us there. As we flew, he told Huell about his desire to help the people of Georgia, who had been left without the most basic medicines and medical supplies in the wake of the Soviet Union's downfall.

We arrived late at the Dallas airport, where we picked up Hayden McElroy and got back into the air for the last leg to Florida. After a long night of travel, we landed and transferred to a Boeing 727 jet that had been waiting for us for hours. Sixteen thousand pounds of medications were already on the plane, along with trauma surgeon Trish Blair, who had devised the plan to get the supplies to Georgia. Dr. Blair was the sister of Jim Blair, who couldn't make the trip himself but had helped finance it. We were also joined by several pilots, who I later learned were there to take over for one another as each pilot fatigued on the long, long flight to Tbilisi.

In an in-flight interview with Huell, Dr. Blair explained her role as the founder and president of A Call to Serve (ACTS), the first humanitarian and development organization to work in Georgia after the collapse of the Soviet Union. Dr. Blair and ACTS volunteers had gathered the medical supplies onboard from around the country; these

Huell interviews Dr. Trish Blair.

included bottles of perfectly good insulin that couldn't be used in the United States because their labels had been applied upside down. She had been working in Georgia for some time and told Huell of her great concern for its people, especially the children.

The pilots sure had their hands full on that flight. Our older 727 had been designed for shorter-range flights, not an intercontinental mission. The plane had to land in Newfoundland, Ireland, and Turkey to refuel, and we were allowed to disembark only once, in Istanbul, to stretch our legs. By the time we arrived in Tbilisi, Georgia, it was around 2 a.m. We landed on a runway with no lights, about seven hours late, and I hadn't slept a wink.

A delegation of some forty people (including generals, dignitaries, and hospital personnel who had been expecting us at seven in the evening) was waiting to greet us. They piled us into cars and whisked us off to a hotel where, much to our surprise, they had set up a banquet in our honor. They fed us well, and straight vodka flowed out of pitchers set on the tables. Harry, allergic to alcohol, passed Huell his share of vodka, which Huell drank, as any polite guest would.

The banquet, called Supra by the delegation, was grand, but by 5 a.m. Huell and I were exhausted. We went to our rooms and slept for an hour before we were rousted out of bed for the shoot. We were beat, and Huell had a big headache—we just wanted to sleep a few minutes more! But we were there to shoot a show, so out we went.

Our first scene began with Huell touring a burn center that was filled with many terribly injured children. He interviewed the staff, who were struggling to care for the children with the meager medications and supplies they had on hand. The situation was pitiful, and the picture looked gray and washed out through my viewfinder. Huell came over and said, "Louie, there's no story for me to take back home. I can't make the story I was thinking of from this." That was saying a lot, as Huell was capable of creating a good story from just about any situation put in front of him.

So the show we intended to shoot fell apart, and we were in the former Soviet Union, thousands of miles from home, without a viable story. Huell asked me if I had any ideas about what to do. I remembered what he was great at: interviewing people in the street. I suggested that we visit a market and see what was there. He agreed, and off we went with our English-speaking guide to see what was happening in the streets of Tbilisi.

What Huell and I witnessed in those city streets was disheartening, to say the least. The Soviet Union had collapsed two years prior, in December of 1991, and the result was fifteen separate countries that had been dependent on centralized planning and supplies coming from Moscow. Though Georgia was one of the countries to gain its freedom, its economy was in shambles.

The market that our guide picked was outdoors on a busy street

Huell interviews Harry Thomason.

bordered by a train station on one side. It was teeming with people buying and trading food and merchandise. Vendors sat behind make-shift stands that looked like orange crates, selling anything they could: light bulbs, bars of laundry soup, potatoes. We even came upon one desperate man trying his hardest to sell an armload of fox pelts to a passing crowd that paid him no attention.

Huell walked up to a man standing in front of a round tank mounted on wheels, with a pair of used shoes for sale propped against it. Our guide told Huell that the tank held homemade beer and invited him to taste it. Though he was always game to try things, including alcoholic beverages, even he had to hesitate at the offer. Against his better judg-ment, he agreed and was handed a glass of beer. He tasted it and made a small sour face. "It sure tastes different," he said. I admired him for not spitting it out.

Huell talks to a Georgian bread baker.

Our guide told Huell that there were no buses; only the subway was running. Most of the city's electricity was out, which explained the candlelight in the hotel banquet room. He compared Georgia to America during the Great Depression: everything had ceased to work, and people were unable to meet their basic needs.

It was like that everywhere we went. Yet the people were polite, courteous, and friendly. A woman in an indoor market, for example, offered Huell free Georgian-style baked bread that she had for sale. Huell tried to pay for it, but she refused money; the bread was a gift to him. He insisted, giving the money to our guide and asking him to make sure she accepted it. There was joy in her voice as she thanked Huell, so grateful to have the money.

By that time, Huell had just about had it with the depressing market shots. Still trying to salvage the show, he asked our guide to take us someplace else that could be of interest.

We shot monuments and buildings as we drove around the city, and we found a few people on the sidewalk in front of a foreign-language institute. Huell asked a sour-looking young woman what she thought of the current state of affairs in Georgia. She said flatly, "There are no places to have fun here. Just go back to America."

Huell looked back at the camera and shook his head, trying to make light of her comment, but I could see he was getting close to the end of his rope trying to get something positive for the show. He interviewed a few more people, most of whom were more optimistic than that woman, but, at the end of a long and difficult day, he gave up and told our guide to take us back to the hotel. I was thankful that he'd pulled the plug, but I felt bad that even after all our efforts, we still didn't have a show.

And the day wasn't over yet. When we arrived at our hotel, the greatly hospitable Georgians (who had set up the 2 a.m. party in our honor) were waiting for us with another gathering and dinner. As tired as we were, how could we refuse? The banquet hall was filled with endless food, drink, and good cheer. We learned that the Georgians had made a considerable effort to cobble together the food for our dinner—they wanted to show us kindness and friendship even though they had so little to share.

The air in the room grew hazy and reeked of the cigarettes everyone seemed to be smoking. We were anxious to leave, and, after some time, Dr. Blair took us all back to the airport. We were accompanied by some of the people who'd initially greeted us upon our arrival at the airport, so it was a grand send-off. We said our goodbyes to Dr. Blair and the Georgians and plopped back into our seats. It was after seven in the evening, and after just one day in Georgia, we were headed home.

The engines started up, and the pilots requested to taxi to the take-off point. But the takeoff didn't happen—the airplane stayed in its spot on the tarmac. After a short while, the pilots disembarked and walked over to Dr. Blair. They told her that the air traffic controller, who had identified himself as a private in the army, was refusing to let the airplane take off.

I couldn't believe our run of bad luck. All our trouble with the delays in getting there, and then the shoot, and now this? But Dr. Blair, who'd worked with and around these kinds of situations during her time in Georgia, gathered Harry, Hayden, and our pilots and marched right up and into the tower. There, according to Harry, they found not only the army private, but two Russian women who told the group that even though the Russians no longer ruled Georgia, they still commanded the airport—and the airplane was not taking off.

Dr. Blair demanded that the airplane be allowed to leave, but the three refused. So she got on the phone and called the minister of health, getting him out of bed, and explained the situation. She handed the phone to the private.

"You will let the plane go," the minister said.

The private, not believing the voice on the other end of the phone really was that of the minister of health, argued. "Anyway, you are not my boss," he finally said, handing the phone back.

But to his surprise, after some time, the actual minister of health showed up in the tower and chewed out the young man, ordering him to let the airplane take off. But the private and his muscle of Russian women stuck to their guns. They controlled the airport, and there would be no takeoff. The frustrated minister left. Just after he departed, the Russians said there might be a way of solving the problem. If the Americans could come up with $10,000 for a landing fee, they'd let the plane leave. In this poor economy, three entrepreneurs had found a way to get rich quick.

No one had that much money, so they called the State Department and explained that the Russians were demanding $10,000 in cash. The State Department folks said they'd look into it and would call back. With the Russians content to wait, Harry, Hayden, Dr. Blair, and the pilots returned to the tarmac.

The pilots, all former military-aircraft jockeys, separated themselves and talked earnestly over a map. One of them showed the others something on the map, and they nodded their heads in agreement. They walked over to Harry and Hayden and showed them the map.

"Here's the drill," one of the pilots said. "The Russians took their fighter aircraft back to Russia, so they don't have any planes in the area." He ran his finger across the map to Russia. "We know it will take at least forty minutes for them to scramble the jets out here. Turkey's airspace is only twenty or thirty minutes away," he said, pointing to Turkey. He looked up at Harry and Hayden. "What we're going to do is take off and get into Turkish airspace before the Russians can get their fighter jets here."

He presented the idea as a declaration, but his eyes asked if they agreed with his daring plan. They said they liked the idea, seeing that the timeline could work, with the only alternative being sitting on the tarmac for who knows how long, perhaps even creating an international incident. Now they had to come up with a story about the money that the Russians would believe.

They devised a story that the State Department had agreed to pay the $10,000 and were on their way to the airport with the cash. They radioed the tower with the fake news, telling the Russians that the money was in a car just outside the airport. And since the cash would arrive at the tower shortly, the pilots asked if they could taxi the 727 to the end of the runway, so they could take off after the money was in the Russians' hands. In their excitement over their impending riches, the Russians agreed.

The pilot taxied to the runway, waited a few seconds, then pushed the throttle forward. The old plane shuddered as its engines spooled up and began rolling the old jet down the runway, gaining speed. The trio in the tower saw what was happening and got on the radio, shouting and cursing at the pilots, demanding that they stop. But the 727 passed the tower, lifted into the air, and got into Turkey's airspace before Russian jets could get to the airplane. What an experience!

All of this happened without Huell and me knowing the full story. My hat is off to Harry, Hayden, and the pilots for coming up with their daring plan to get us safely home.

We flew back on the same route, only in reverse. The trip seemed to take even longer this time, perhaps because I was so anxious to get home, and now that I was aware of the many stops the plane would be making, I counted them off one by one.

The best part of the trip home was that I got to sit in the cockpit with the pilots. From time to time they'd leave the cockpit and pop into the main cabin for breaks and snacks, so I struck up conversations with them. In the cockpit, I chatted with the pilots and even flew the plane—no, not really, but the experience was fun, and it kept my mind off the fact that I was more tired than I'd ever been in my life.

A mere two days after the beginning of our journey to Tbilisi, we landed in Florida in the good old US of A. I tell you, it felt great to be back on American soil. After dropping off Mr. McElroy, whom we had picked up in Dallas, we flew straight to Burbank Airport, where we said goodbye to Harry. Huell and I had traveled halfway around the world to spend a single day on the ground—and for all that trouble, we didn't have anything useful in the can to make a show.

Yet we knew we had gained something valuable. If the idea of the show hadn't fallen apart, we wouldn't have ventured into Tbilisi's marketplaces, and we would have come back to America unaware of the terrible economic toll the collapse of the Soviet Union had taken on the Georgian people. It was a tragedy we had witnessed and captured firsthand, one that few Americans knew about at that time.

HUELL IN CONTROL

California's Gold was Huell's baby all the way. He developed the idea, got Wells Fargo to sponsor it, and had all the California PBS stations guarantee they'd run the series before they even saw it. Given my camera work on the *Videolog* "Elephant Man" show, he knew he could trust me to capture his vision for *California's Gold*.

Many ideas for the show came from Huell's meetings with his production staff and from audience feedback. Fans from all over California would suggest places and events to visit—usually a fair, festival, or historical celebration. Sometimes, he just wanted to go out, explore, and film something that captivated him. As owner and host of *California's Gold*, he had the final say on what we shot.

All the equipment I used belonged to Huell, down to the batteries in my camera gear. I'd go out shopping with him and he'd tell me to buy whatever gear I needed, never balking at the price. After all, it wasn't like we were shooting brain surgery—we made the most of what we had, and not even the most expensive gear in the world could have rivaled our teamwork and passion for the shows we created.

Huell was also very involved in the editing process. In the show files are pages upon pages of handwritten notes describing cuts, segues, where the music comes in and goes out, his narration, and various scene lengths down to the millisecond. In some files, Huell's editing notes are just about all that's there. Outside of my involvement as an engineer, only a couple of trusted editors were allowed to have creative input.

As you know, my job was to be behind the camera, and I never had the slightest interest in being in front of it. But Huell did manage to get a shot of me in one show. We were doing a show in San Pedro on master divers, the guys who go down deep in diving bells. The plan was for him to go down in a bell and for me to shoot the bell as it popped to the surface. The hatch would open, revealing Huell after his adventure down below.

He went down in the bell, and when it came back up, the hatch opened and out popped Huell, grinning while taking a picture of me with a small camera he had concealed. He thought it was funny, taking a picture of me taking a picture of him, and he edited that into the show. That was my first and last television cameo.

Although viewers never knew my face, Huell was always generous when it came to recognizing my contributions to *California's Gold*. He referred to us as a team, telling viewers that I was responsible for the look of the show. As a matter of fact, he once said to me, "You know, Louie, people come up to me all the time and ask me about you, wanting to know who you are. I hear it everywhere I go."

I was tickled, and asked, "What do you tell them?"

He laughed and said, "I point to someone random and say, 'That guy is Louie,' and they go over and talk to him."

But Huell was human like all of us, and a couple of times, he let his ego get in the way. A few times when I was with him, we'd see fans coming over, and of course he'd expect them to gather around and gush over him. They gushed over him all right—but when they saw me with my camera, they'd ask if I was Louie, and sometimes they'd leave him to gather around me instead, shaking my hand and telling me they always wanted to know who that guy Louie was that Huell talked to. He wasn't always happy about losing the attention of fans.

One time when we were together, Huell was approached by a few fans—but when someone saw me and told the others who I was, they left him to talk with me. When they went back to Huell and told him they'd finally gotten to meet Louie, he stared at me, not pleased. I threw my arms up and shrugged my shoulders. "Don't look at me like that, Huell," I said. "You created this monster." It took him a bit of time to get over it, but he did. He always did.

In all the years we were together, Huell never submitted a *California's Gold* show for an Emmy award. Because I thought we had shot some outstanding shows that were worthy of Emmy consideration, I once asked him why he never considered submission. He carefully considered his response, and then said, "Louie, I'm afraid to lose, that's why."

I don't think his fear was due to a lack of confidence in the programs. He identified a lot with *California's Gold*—it was a reflection of his vision, his creativity, himself. If the show lost to any program he thought of as lesser, I firmly believe that he would have considered himself a loser.

But there was one thing he did for me that led to recognition for *California's Gold*. Impressed with my work on the episode, he suggested that I submit the "Golden Gate Bridge" shoot for an award from the Press Photographers Association of Greater Los Angeles. I submitted the show—and it won! It felt great to win an award for shooting a *California's Gold* show, and I was grateful to Huell for encouraging me to submit it.

To this day, I wish he had submitted *California's Gold* for Emmy consideration. I think we would have swept the field year after year. But, as I said, Huell was in control—and he always had the final say.

Enjoying menudo with Louie's mother, Josephina Fuerte.

BEYOND
CALIFORNIA'S GOLD

Huell never stopped thinking. He came up with new show ideas constantly, and many of them were outstanding. One of his most successful was 1993's *Visiting with Huell Howser*, which we called *Visiting* for short. It began its nineteen-year run about two years after he'd created *California's Gold*. *Visiting* was a KCET production, which meant the station owned the show but Huell had creative control, and I did all the shooting.

Whereas the backbone of *California's Gold* was the beauty and history of the state and its people, *Visiting* told more personal stories. It centered on the diverse communities in Southern California, with many of the shows featuring the comings and goings of regular people. Since most episodes took place in and around Los Angeles, we could usually complete a shoot in a single day.

Huell's big appetite and love of food led us to shoot quite a few shows at restaurants. One show told the story of menudo, the Mexican tripe soup rumored to possess curative powers for hangovers. The first part of that episode was shot at Juanita's Foods, the largest maker of canned menudo in the country. The second part was shot at a Mexican restaurant that I liked in Colton, a small town next to San Bernardino.

I told my mother that we were going to shoot there, and she got so excited she asked if she could come along, promising that she'd just sit and watch to see what I do.

I said, "Mom, after all this time, you don't know what I do?"

She said, "I know, I know, but I have never seen you do it!"

Well, she arrived at the restaurant all dressed up and looking so nice that Huell decided to interview her for the program. He sat next to her at a table with a big bowl in front of him as she explained all of menudo's subtleties. Filming Huell's first taste of the mythical Mexican soup was great fun, and I'll never forget his thoughtfulness toward my mother that day. It was such a thrill for her.

Huell was continually creating new shows for KCET. He and his staff were champs at uncovering interesting subjects all over California, and viewers loved the shows. In addition to *Visiting* and *California's Gold*, Huell developed *California's Golden Parks* and several one-hour specials, including a tour of Frank Sinatra's Palm Springs home. During our time together, we shot hundreds of shows, traveling everywhere from Death Valley and the Sierra Nevada to San Diego and San Francisco.

Huell also created shows that he personally shot without me as his cameraman. One of them was a series called *Hot Summer Nights*. From the early evening to around 2 a.m., he took a small handheld camera out into the streets of Los Angeles to capture the feel of the city at night. He met people everywhere he went and interviewed them; these were people who probably would never have been on TV if it weren't for Huell. It said a lot about his belief that everyone has a story to tell.

Of course, not all of Huell's program ideas worked out. One of them was called *The Bench*. The idea behind it was to go to a park, sit on a bench—Huell with his microphone and me with my camera—and just wait for someone to walk by. He would approach the person in an attempt to get some interesting dialogue going, such as why he or she was in the park that day—anything to flesh out a good personal story.

Huell knew he was good at interviewing, and maybe he thought that was enough to get complete strangers to open up to him with compelling, watchable stories for no good reason. On our first shoot of *The Bench*, we videotaped people who came up to us, perhaps out of curiosity about the two friendly-looking guys just sitting there with a mic and camera. That turned out so-so. The second time out, we were at a big park, with no bench in sight. We set up anyway and waited for someone to come by, but after a while Huell just walked right up to a man and began talking to him.

"Why are you in the park in the middle of the day?" Huell asked. "Aren't you supposed to be at work?"

Apparently, the questions didn't sit well with the man, but Huell got some kind of interview on tape with him. After the shoot, I asked, "Huell, the name of the program is *The Bench*. Where's the bench?"

He just laughed. "Louie," he said good-naturedly, "I don't know if this bench thing is going to work."

Although those two episodes of *The Bench* went on the air, we didn't shoot many more. With neither theme nor structure, the show was completely dependent on the hope that random people walking through a park would have interesting stories to share. As it turned out, all the interviewing talent in the world couldn't turn every stranger into a confidant—with or without a bench.

HUELL
BEHIND THE SCENES

A lot of people didn't know that Huell was afraid of heights—but he showed it on only a few shoots. If you listen carefully during shows that involve heights, you'll hear him groping for words and frequently saying that he is *"way* up there."

One such shoot was at the Marine Corps Air Station in Santa Ana, famous for its huge wooden blimp hangars built back in 1942. We were in awe of the huge size of the buildings! Huell came up with the idea of filming the hangars up in the roof trusses so viewers could get a better idea of their enormous size. We slowly climbed hundreds of feet up a steep, knee-aching stairway, only to discover that the only way to get around on the trusses was by walking over narrow wooden catwalks that led from one to the next.

Our guide took off through the trusses, and Huell began walking behind him, holding onto the rail with a death grip. The guide walked the narrow catwalks as easily as if he were on a sidewalk. Huell, on the other hand, was nervous—and I could hear it.

As he was making his way along the aerial walkway, Huell said, "I assume it's sturdy, 'cause I gotta tell you, it's a little strange right now." He followed that with, "This is the original wood, and I assume it's sturdy?"

Our guide assured Huell again and again that the catwalk was safe, but by the sound of his voice, I don't think Huell believed him.

I have a fear of heights, too, but staying focused on the act of filming saved me from worrying about slipping and falling to the concrete floor far below. Shooting Huell and the hangar left no time for distractions—but poor Huell had to do the walk-and-talk to give his viewers perspective on the hangar's immense size. I tell you, it was a relief for both of us to be back on the ground.

Another show that revealed his uneasiness with heights is the *Visiting* story we did on the then-tallest building in Los Angeles. We were up seventy-three stories, interviewing the window washers who had the task of cleaning the building's thousands of windows from top to bottom. A narrow ramp connected the main building to a window-cleaning platform that telescoped outward, leaving a space between the scaffold and the building. Looking down from the walkway, you could see tiny people on the sidewalk far, far below.

Accompanying Huell was a group of people associated with the

Huell working hard to be brave up in the catwalks in the Marine Corps blimp hangar.

high-rise, and among them was a woman in heels. She casually strode across the walkway and looked back at Huell, her expression saying, "C'mon Huell, you can do it." He hesitated, and then tentatively followed her lead—as if he were walking on eggshells. Once he was securely on the scaffold, he warily advised the operator, "Any sudden movement and I get real nervous." Boy oh boy, did he look relieved that he had made it across safely.

Another quirk of Huell's that many fans will recall was his habit of repeating something a guest said, especially if what he'd heard intrigued him. Often, his astonished repetition would leave a guest with no other option than to politely confirm what he or she had just said.

We were filming up in Taft in Central California, doing an episode on the historic oil fields in the area, when there was talk of something Huell needed to see. So we changed the setup and I shot Huell among a small group of people walking along a country road. Someone in the group told Huell about Lakeview Gusher, a nearby oil well that, in the early 1900s, spewed millions of gallons of oil into the air for eighteen months. Later, someone else repeated the story to him, also referring to the eighteen months. When they got to the site of the well, Huell asked with great Huell enthusiasm, "You mean there was oil coming out of here uncontrollably for *eighteen months*?" And, of course, everyone confirmed that yes, indeed, that's exactly what had happened.

The all-time *California's Gold* record of Huell and his guest repeating themselves was during a show we did on Santa Rosa Island. I was shooting Huell and a park ranger as they hiked around looking at the island's native plants. While they were inspecting a flowering prickly pear cactus, another plant caught the ranger's attention. "And this plant is called the Lemonade Berry," he said, pointing to the plant in question.

Instantly, Huell's interest was piqued. "The Lemonade Berry?"

"Yes," the ranger said. "We call it the Lemonade Berry because—"

In his excitement, Huell cut him off as he strode toward the berry; I followed dutifully with my camera. He said, "What do you mean? This thing is called the *Lemonade Berry*?"

And the ranger said, "Yes. This is called the Lemonade Berry."

The five mentions of that plant was Huell's *California's Gold* all-time repeating record, but that was just part of Huell's charm.

HUELL'S ZEST FOR LIFE

Huell didn't let anything get in the way of having fun, and mixing business and pleasure was part of his modus operandi. Often he'd meet in advance with people who were going to be on the show, to help get the lay of the land and get a sense of what he wanted to shoot, and sometimes, if he hit it off with the people in question, those meetings would go past midnight.

Early one morning, I was jolted awake by a loud and insistent banging on the door of the room next to mine. It was 4 a.m., and I could tell that Huell was the culprit. He couldn't find his key, and I guess he figured the door would open if he hit it long and hard enough. After a time, the pounding stopped and I fell back asleep. At least I knew he was alive.

The next morning around 8 a.m., I saw him at the shoot location. His body was there (nursing a cup of coffee), but his spirit appeared to be back in his hotel room, asleep under the covers. As bad as he looked, I knew him well enough that I still could have fun with him.

"It looks like you partied hard last night," I said. "Did the meeting run late?"

He didn't say anything, just drank his coffee and looked at me with sleepy eyes. But Huell, always the showman, got it together and when the time came for the camera to roll, he held up the mic with a smile, and did the show just fine.

Another time we were on location shooting a *California's Gold* story when Huell showed up after a night of partying with his new-found pals. I walked over to him, and in a ragged voice barely above a whisper, he said, "Hi, Louie." His shoulders sagged, his face the color of an unripe tomato. He peered at me through narrow slits. The man was in major discomfort, probably thinking that death would be a nice alternative to filming that day. He met my eye, and I thought he was going to say something about how we should get the day's shooting going.

"Louie," he said, "take the day off. We can shoot this tomorrow."

I packed up my gear and went into town to see the sights, while Huell made up for the sleep he'd missed the night before. The next day we got another good *California's Gold* in the bag.

Liquid refreshments weren't Huell's only fuel of choice. He also liked to eat. No, let me take that back—he *loved* to eat. And boy, did he love his steaks. On those rare occasions when we ate dinner together, he usually chose the restaurant, which more than likely would be a steakhouse. I'm a pretty light eater, and I haven't had red meat in more than forty years. But Huell would always order a big piece of meat with mashed potatoes, gravy, and all the fixings. While we talked, I'd have my salad, and he'd make that steak disappear.

Something that I'll never forget about his eating habits happened during many of our shooting trips in Northern California. Huell just loved to visit the In-N-Out Burger at the Highway 41 Kettleman City exit. He'd get excited as we approached the turnoff, like a little boy who couldn't wait to open his birthday presents. He'd order fries and burgers, double-doubles, triple patties—whatever looked good to him at the time, downing it all with gusto. I began to think the real reason we did so many shoots up north was so he could make that stop at his favorite I-5 In-N-Out.

As you can probably guess, the two-part "See's Candies" show that aired in July of 1998 was a sweet slice of heaven for Huell. For the first part, we went up to San Francisco to shoot at one of the original See's locations, and he got to sample all the delicious chocolates he wanted.

Trying the merch at See's Candies.

I happened to notice that he wore a loose blue sweater that day. He may have worn it because of the cool San Francisco weather, but given how much candy he ate, it might have been a strategic move.

For the second part of the series, we shot at the big See's factory in Los Angeles. I shot Huell's tour of the factory for a good part of the day, following him through the candy-making process. See's makes a great variety of chocolate confections, and Huell cheerily sampled them as he went along. It's no surprise that he ended the episode by eating a piece right off the assembly line—See's is a California legend, famous for its chocolates, and for Huell to get a tour of the factory and sample just about all of them was clearly a dream come true for the big guy.

Even with a sweet tooth like his, Huell was an athletic and imposing man. He exercised constantly in the early days *California's Gold*, which gave him stamina for the many physically demanding shoots we went on—we climbed mountains, swirled in whitewater rapids, and often hiked for hours just to get our stories. During those years, he always wore his short-sleeved shirts tucked in to show his slim waist, great biceps, and big chest. Pay attention to the way he interviewed people in the early episodes of *California's Gold*. You'll see him standing sideways to the camera, flexing those guns as he leans in, holding his mic in one hand with the other hand on his hip, showing off his fine physique.

By late 2000, years of traveling had begun to take their toll. Huell changed his hair, letting it grow a bit longer so it was fashioned into small waves. I called it his "Greek God" phase: interesting and different, but considerably grayer, just like mine. In our last year working together on *California's Gold*, we were shooting at Big Bear in the San Bernardino Mountains when it hit me that he was wearing his shirt hanging out. There was no tight T-shirt tucked into his pants, no showing of his big biceps. Huell's grand appetite was finally catching up with him, and of course, age was catching up with both of us.

One more thing you may not know about Huell is that he was gay. He was completely private about it, and the public had no idea until someone outed him very publicly after his death—something that would have made him very unhappy. His sexuality didn't mean a hill of beans to me, and it hasn't mattered a bit to his fans, either. The wonder, adventure, and entertainment of his shows are what's important. He showed you the marvelous grandeur of California, from the snow-covered Sierra Nevada to the Pacific's sandy shores. Perhaps he even inspired you to go see the sights for yourself.

That's what it was all about, all those *California's Gold* shows and the many others he created for your enjoyment. His was a genuine and insatiable curiosity about California and its people, and he had a deep-felt desire to show the world the things he loved about his adopted state. His legacy is reflected in his extraordinary talent for compelling ordinary people to open up and share their stories with others. That's what we all remember, and cherish, about Huell.

Huell with a Pink's Huell Dog.

HUELL'S IMPACT

Huell attracted people like a magnet attracts iron filings. No matter where we were, at an airport, a restaurant, or even the gas station, fans would recognize him and congregate around him. At six-foot-four, he stood a head above most of the crowd, but even if he'd been an average-size guy, his warmth and gregarious personality would have drawn people to him. At times, he'd seem genuinely surprised and somewhat flustered with all the adulation. His "Aw, shucks" approach may have been a way to deal with being swamped by people, but I think he was often genuinely taken aback with the attention.

As you can imagine, he got quite a lot of letters from fans detailing their admiration for both him and the programs, but the ones that were the most special to him were the ones about *California's Gold*. He loved hearing from people who'd built ships at Richmond's Kaiser Shipyards during World War II, and from the construction workers who'd helped create the Shasta Dam. His programs touched their lives and awakened their memories.

Since his passing, thousands of people have gathered at Chapman University, home to the Huell Howser Archives, to honor him and his work. At one of these gatherings, I met an enthusiastic and fun group called the HuellAgains, who wore T-shirts with a bold *HuellAgains* splashed across the front. Their goal was to visit all of the *California's Gold* and *Visiting with Huell Howser* shooting locations throughout the state, sharing their adventures with one another to keep the memory of those shows alive. They still felt that close to him.

I saw many members of the HuellAgains again in Palm Springs in October of 2015. They'd made the trip to the desert to see the unveiling of Huell's star on the Palm Springs Walk of Stars; I'd been asked to speak at the ceremony. The HuellAgains even gave me one of their colorful T-shirts that they wore so proudly that day.

At the dedication, I shared a few stories about Huell and our adventures together, and then had the privilege of unveiling his star. It was quite an honor. Huell was a genuine, one-of-a-kind guy. And not only did he make viewers' lives richer with his shows about California, but he also had a positive impact in many other ways.

For example, sometimes Huell took on the role of crusader. He particularly liked to use *Visiting* to advocate for causes he believed in. During the Los Angeles County budget crisis of 1993, Huell learned that the Los Angeles Board of Supervisors was considering closing fifty of the county's eighty-seven libraries to help balance the budget. So Huell developed a *Visiting* episode called "Library," for which he interviewed patrons at a county library who talked about how much they needed and enjoyed its services. "We need the taxpayers of Los Angeles County to hear this," he said. "What kind of society are we if we close libraries?"

The last shot in the show was a large group of children. "Think of the kids," he said, warning that LA County's children would be irreparably harmed if the libraries closed. Huell's appeal helped the cause: all the libraries that were slated to be closed were kept open.

WHAT HUELL DID FOR SMALL BUSINESSES

To me, there's no question that Huell was the best booster that California has ever had. Every time he visited and then showcased a park, fair, monument, or special event in the state, there'd be a surge of visitors who wanted to experience what he'd showed them. He was the Pied Piper of California.

Huell never did a show about a location or business to deliberately punch up its sales. That was the incidental result of his interest in whatever he was exploring. After a visit from Huell aired on TV, new customers would show up to that establishment in droves, typically pushing sales sky high in the weeks, months, and even years after the show aired.

Take, for instance, Huell's *Visiting* interview with John Nese, owner of Galco's Old World Grocery. This specialty store in the Highland Park neighborhood of Los Angeles carries virtually every kind of soda you've ever imagined, including old-time favorites that many of us re-

Exploring the beverage array at Galco's Old World Grocery.

member from our childhoods. Huell had a great time talking with John and his family, who run the store together.

Before the show aired, Huell called John to alert him that a lot of people were going to show up at his door. "I want you to be ready," he said. "You're going to be busier than you've ever been."

John stocked the shelves in anticipation of a good sales day—and was shocked when the huge crowd that showed up emptied his store in no time flat. "Huell was the best thing that ever happened to small businesses," said John.

Huell used to stop by now and then to talk with John and see how things were going with him and the store. He didn't forget the people in his shows who became his friends.

At the Galco shoot, I overheard a customer say to Huell that he'd always wanted to meet him, but he also wanted to see who Louie was, the guy Huell was always calling to when he wanted to get a close-up of something. So Huell called me over and introduced me, and the customer exclaimed how he was so pleased to meet me and talked about liking my camera work. I'm a pretty shy person, and to this day I still hope he wasn't terribly disappointed with my quiet way of saying thanks—especially after meeting Huell, who was so outgoing—but he seemed glad that he'd finally met the man behind the camera.

Another shoot we did for *Visiting* was at Stan's Donuts in Westwood, near UCLA. Huell had done a mini-story on the doughnut shop when he'd worked with Ralph Story at KCBS. Over the years, he had kept in touch with the owner, Stan Berman, and he thought Stan's deserved a good half hour of doughnut airtime.

So we shot an episode there, and Huell ate his doughnuts and had a lot of fun with Stan and his customers. Before the show aired, Huell called Stan and told him to get ready for an increase in business. Stan said that on the day the show went on the air, business went up by twenty-five percent—and that's just for one day, at a simple doughnut shop in Westwood.

During that shoot, Huell sampled a doughnut topped with peanut butter and chocolate. He loved it, and because of his rave review on camera, Stan named it in his honor. To this day, you can order the Huell at Stan's Donuts, and you'll get that peanut butter and chocolate delight.

Stan has often said that people come into his shop early in the morning on a "Huell run," making Stan's Donuts their first stop on a day of visiting places Huell had been to. A later stop might be lunch at Pink's Hot Dogs or Philippe's for a French-dip sandwich, and they'd often finish the Huell run at Galco's to buy some unusual sodas or at Fosselman's to have some ice cream.

Stan says there's camaraderie among the owners of the businesses that Huell celebrated, and that they stay in touch with one another. They even send customers who are on a Huell run to other stores in their special club.

Pink's Hot Dogs in Los Angeles was one of Huell's favorite places

Stan takes the mic while Huell tries the goods.

Huell with Gloria Pink at Pink's Hot Dogs.

to eat, and it's another business that benefitted from Huell's exposure. He loved their dogs and had been a regular customer for some time before we did our two shoots there. Every year on their anniversary, Pink's celebrates with a charity event, pricing their hot dogs for that year. For example, on their seventy-fifth anniversary, they sold seventy-five cent hot dogs for seventy-five minutes. All the money earned goes to the charity choice of whichever celebrity Pink's invited that year to help draw people to the event.

Though all of Pink's celebrity hosts—actors, athletes, politicians—have drawn large crowds to the event over the years, their numbers paled in comparison to the year Huell hosted the celebration. More than a thousand people showed up, jamming the sidewalks for blocks. One family came all the way from Fresno just to meet Huell. That family's wish was granted, and the owner, Richard Pink, said Huell made it a point to talk with them.

Richard said that Huell helped put Pink's on the map, inspiring travelers from all over the state (and the country) to visit the simple hot dog stand. "It's like a pilgrimage, people coming from distant locations because Huell visited us and liked our dogs," he said. "His credibility was so strong. People believed him."

For our second shoot there, Pink's created a special hot dog for Huell, and they presented it to him as a surprise. Made with two dogs, mustard, onions, and chili, it was dubbed the Huell Dog—and I could see that he was truly honored. It remains a popular menu item. If you go to Pink's, look for the sign shaped like California on the menu wall, with a picture and label for the Huell Dog. Order it, and think about Huell enjoying his own special dog with that signature grin on his face.

Of all the businesses we shot, Broguiere's Farm Fresh Dairy in Montebello held a special place in Huell's heart. During our first of several shoots at the dairy, I could see that Huell and owner Ray Broguiere had

Broguiere's Farm Fresh Dairy.

hit it off immediately. They joked and laughed and matched each other's personalities—there was never a moment of dead air between the two.

Ray said that when Huell called him up one day and said he'd like to do a shoot at the dairy, he thought one of his friends was pulling a prank on him. It turns out someone had called Huell and told him about the dairy and its famous chocolate milk and seasonal eggnog. It took some time, but Huell finally convinced Ray that he was the genuine article, and they agreed on a day for the shoot.

Huell and I toured the operation to plot setups and places to shoot. He was introduced to the rich, creamy chocolate milk and was hooked, drinking bottles of it between takes. He really got into the spirit of the shoot, signing autographs for delivery drivers and carrying milk to customers waiting in their cars. In the camera's viewfinder, I saw the astonished looks on customers' faces as they pointed and mouthed, "Hey, that's Huell Howser!" as he cheerfully walked out with their order.

One lady called her son and told him that Huell Howser was serving her at the dairy. He didn't believe her and hung up. Huell being Huell, asked for her phone and called the son back. He said, "Your mom is telling the truth. I'm Huell Howser, and you'd better believe your mother!"

Before the first Broguiere's show went on the air, Huell once again offered his sage advice, urging Ray to prepare for a lot of new customers. Sure enough, the very next day the place was overrun, with cars lined up for blocks.

Our second Broguiere's shoot took place during the holidays. Huell wanted to see how the dairy made its famous eggnog, so Ray took him through the process. The eggnog had a great reputation, much like the company's chocolate milk, but it was available only toward the end of the year. Huell thoroughly enjoyed the many bottles he drank between setups.

The third time we shot an episode at the dairy, Ray presented Huell with a special milk bottle he'd had made with Huell's picture on it. He joked that the bottle would make Huell famous and keep him from ever getting lost—but really, it was to thank him for his friendship and what he'd done for the dairy. Huell was excited and touched, and almost at a loss for words when he saw the bottle—and I rarely saw the man at a loss for words.

Huell often visited the dairy on his own, calling Ray to say he was getting off the freeway and asking for directions, as if he'd never been there. They really enjoyed each other's company, and Huell always had fun helping at the dairy and surprising customers when he served them their order. Ray said Huell even talked with him about retiring from television about two to three years before he passed away, saying that everything comes to an end.

Toward the end of 2012, Ray said that Huell had stopped dropping by, and they talked only by phone occasionally. One day in December, Huell's close friend Ryan Morris came by the dairy, saying that Huell would like some eggnog and chocolate milk in the bottles with Huell's picture on them. Ray asked how Huell was and why he hadn't come by for a long time, and Ryan deflected the question and said he'd be in touch later. (As I discuss later in this book, Huell was extremely private about his personal life, and his health.) A couple of weeks later, Ryan called Ray at 6 a.m. to tell him that Huell had died of prostate cancer. Ray's name was on a short list that Huell had made of people he wanted notified when he died. Truly, he was Huell's friend.

Broguiere's Dairy is still a popular destination for Huell's fans. To this day, whenever one of Huell's programs featuring his dairy goes on the air, Ray's business is crowded the next day with people looking to experience all that Huell enjoyed.

PLEDGE DRIVES

California's Gold produced a lot of donations for KCET during its regular pledge drives. Part of PBS at that time, the station depended heavily on viewer donations to fund production of its many wonderful programs. Whenever the station had pledge drives featuring *California's Gold* episodes, Huell was invited to host the evening in the studio. His Tennessee accent, boyish charm, legendary exuberance, and imposing stature made him irresistible to viewers.

When he encouraged viewers to call to show their support for KCET's programs, the sound of ringing phones would flood the background. Every volunteer, like the late, much-beloved Dorothy Kemps, would be answering calls to take pledges, calling for runners to take their handwritten pledge slips for verification before getting right back on the phone to take another pledge. When Huell was on the air, the stage was always filled with noise, action, and excitement, all to raise money for a great cause.

Among all the worthy programs that KCET was airing at that time, the *California's Gold* marathons generated some of the largest donation pledges. I shot those pledge-drive shows myself, a new experience for me, but I soon got into the swing of things. It felt great to see the programs that I'd shot for Huell bring in money to support the station.

Funnily enough, some viewers would call in asking for Louie, Huell's cameraman. There I was, manning a studio camera while they called in, hearing callers asking for me personally. One night, a viewer actually called to pledge $500 if Huell would put me on camera.

I leaned away from the camera viewfinder and shook my head no. *California's Gold* was Huell's show—he was the face of it, and I didn't want to take anything away from him. Besides, I think my refusal to be on camera added a little spice to the show. I mean, people were probably thinking, who is this guy Louie who gets mentioned all the time? The mystique was built into the show, like Carlton the doorman in the TV comedy *Rhoda*—the man you heard on the intercom but never saw.

I liked staying behind the camera for those pledge drives, but if you had told me back then that KCET would one day be organizing a pledge drive for the station featuring book about Huell and me—with my name on the cover, no less—I would have laughed in your face.

But I guess the joke is on me.

LEAVING
CALIFORNIA'S GOLD

I turned forty-nine the year I began shooting *California's Gold* for Huell. I wasn't a young man at the time, but I was a long-distance swimmer and I ran to keep myself in shape. I was strong and felt young, and I thought I could go on forever.

Time, however, has a way of putting you in your place.

It was in my tenth year shooting *California's Gold* and Huell's other shows that I began to feel that I couldn't continue to shoot. I was fifty-nine, and the weight and methods of maneuvering the camera were getting to me. I ached, and I was growing tired of the camera gear and constant travel. I enjoyed the shoots with Huell, but being on the road was beating me up, especially the ten-day road trips we made two to three times a year.

At home, things were different, too. The strain on my marriage was telling. I'd come home after a long trip and feel as if I had to get reacquainted with my wife and kids—even feeling like a stranger at times. One day, I accepted something I'd known deep down for a long time: my marriage was over.

I was heartbroken. Ending a long marriage was the most difficult thing I ever had to do. There were all those good years and good times, and our wonderful kids. You add it all up again and again, and you cry over it and still wonder why you're where you are. There's the deep pain of being estranged from your children when you finally walk away. I love my kids, and I missed them.

So when I finally told Huell I was done, I meant it. I remember it clearly: He was driving the Explorer on the way home from a shoot up north, where he loved to do shows. I had been thinking about how to tell him I wanted out. Ten years of a wonderfully successful run is hard to quit—I mean, you don't get off a winning horse, do you? We'd become a seasoned shooting team, and there were so many more shows to shoot.

I said, "Huell, I'm thinking about retiring from the show. I'm tired of traveling and carrying all that gear. I'm not a kid anymore, and my body's beat. I think it's time for you to start looking for another cameraman." My words caught him completely by surprise. As if he'd only heard that I wanted out, he looked at me and asked, "Louie, why do you want to leave?"

"Huell, I'm tired. I'm tired of traveling, of going in and out of airports. I don't want to do it anymore. I *can't* do it anymore."

Huell drove on, saying nothing for some time, his eyes fixed on the traffic ahead.

At last he said, "I hate to see you go."

"Me too, Huell. I've also been giving some thought to retiring from the station, slowing down, enjoying life."

Again, he grew quiet. Then he thanked me for the shoot we had just done. As we approached KCET'S Sunset Boulevard entrance, I said I'd give him six months to find another cameraman. I couldn't just hang my friend out to dry.

He said that should be enough to find someone, and he thanked me for giving him the extra time.

At the station, I started unloading the gear from the car, and Huell walked into the office to check his messages. He came out, reached for my hand, and shook it.

"Thank you for everything, Louie," he said. Then he walked away.

Five months passed, and no progress was made on hiring a new camera operator. I asked Huell why no one had been brought in to replace me.

And you know what Huell did? The most underhanded, dirtiest thing he could do: offer me more money to stay for six months longer. And even worse, I took it.

At the end of the second six months, he repeated his unconscionable act and offered me even more money. And what do you know—I took that, too.

But the third time the offer came around from Huell (and it did—all kidding aside, I was grateful), no amount of money could override my exhaustion from all that traveling and carrying the camera. I was weary, deep into my bones. And something happened while I was shooting the last *California's Gold* show of the year 2000 that told me it was really and finally time to hang up my gloves.

We were shooting a show in San Francisco called "Emperor and President," and Huell was interviewing someone outdoors. He began walking with the man, and I followed him as I always had, instinctively knowing his every move. He stopped and turned his back to the camera while continuing the interview. At this point, he expected me to circle him as I had done a thousand times before, walking the camera around so I'd end up shooting him from the front. But this time, I kept the camera rolling and didn't move.

I looked at that shot later. It's probably something that most viewers wouldn't even notice, but it said to me that I had lost something that was critical to the look of the show.

After that shoot, I told Huell again that he better find someone soon, because when the next shoot came up, he wouldn't have a cameraman. So that's what he did.

HUELL'S ILLNESS

In December of 2011, my wife, Gloria, and I attended the Annual Engineers Christmas Potluck in the Little Theater at the KCET studios. I had met Gloria at my doctor's office, where she was a nurse, and we fell in love and were married in August of 2004. A few months after our marriage, I retired from KCET, my thirty-two-year career at the studio behind me.

I always looked forward to the potluck, to sit and eat with old friends and talk about what was going on in their lives and at the lot. I was still interested in talking about productions, and I liked to reminisce about KCET's "Golden Age," when we all worked on those creative productions that stretched our abilities and imaginations.

But things were different this time. My former colleagues didn't want to talk about production or the old days. The big topic of the day was the recent sale of the studio lot to the Church of Scientology. The engineers were worried, uncertain of their futures as employees and fearing that the station would downsize and move to a smaller location where they wouldn't be needed. There was a lot of unhappiness on this usually cheerful occasion.

As she mingled at the party, Gloria overheard someone mentioning that Huell wasn't well. Without telling me what she'd heard, she suggested we visit Huell at the office after lunch. I thought that was a great idea, as I hadn't seen him in some time.

We said our goodbyes to our friends and wished them luck, then walked the short distance to the administration building. Just as we arrived at the first floor, the elevator doors began to open—and there in the middle of the elevator appeared Harry Pallenberg, one of Huell's producers. His arms were full of boxes. I was pleasantly surprised to see him, and after we said our hellos, he nodded at the boxes and said they were moving out of their offices.

"Huell's closing everything down. He got an office off the lot, and he's shutting down the KCET offices."

That made sense, because the studios had been sold and Scientology was moving in. I asked Harry if he was going to work with Huell in the new offices, and he said no. That didn't make sense—he'd been with Huell for years. I told Harry I was sorry to see him go, then got in the elevator with Gloria to make our way to Huell's office.

Phil Noyes, Huell's longtime senior producer, was in the office, along with the production coordinator, Ryan Morris. Phil was packing boxes, and Ryan was typing away at the computer. Phil greeted me warmly, and then quickly said, "We've been terminated. Huell got another office in Hollywood."

I was stunned. I noticed that Phil said "we," meaning he was being let go, too. Phil had been with Huell as his senior producer for almost twenty years. Why lay off both Phil and Harry simply because the office was being moved off the lot? Who would produce Huell's shows?

I asked if I really understood what he'd said, that he was not going to go with Huell to the new office. He said, "No, we're done. It's over."

Gloria asked about Huell, saying that she'd heard he was ill. "Yes, he's not well," he said. "If you want to know anything more about that, you'll have to ask Ryan."

I looked over at Ryan, who nodded in agreement. Just then, Harry

came back to the office with the dolly, and he and Phil continued packing the many files, research materials, and objects they had accumu-
lated—the representation of almost twenty years of work.

It seemed like Phil wanted to tell me more about Huell's illness, but
he felt like he had to hold back, even though Huell and I had worked together as friends for so many years. But although the world saw Huell
as a gregarious, exuberant friend, he was actually an extremely private
man. He didn't want anyone knowing what was wrong with him, and
the few people who did know, like Ryan, who was also a close friend of
Huell's, honored his wishes.

As we stood there watching them pack, Phil said there was still a lot
of work to be done on the productions—unfinished shows that needed
narration and editing.

I said, "This is a complete surprise. I expected the show to go on
forever. There are so many things still left to shoot."

He looked at me wistfully and said, "Yeah, I thought forever, too."

That was it. *California's Gold*, *Visiting with Huell Howser*, and all
his other programs were done. No more trips to the far reaches of California to discover its wonders, no more shoots around Southern California to visit places that Huell thought you should see, and no more
meeting people who had fascinating stories to tell.

As I shook their hands, I wished Phil and Harry luck and told them
to call me if they needed anything. I asked Ryan about having lunch
with Huell, and he said he'd ask Huell and get back to me. I wanted to
ask more questions, but the unsettling atmosphere in the room quieted
me. Ryan was clearly respecting Huell's wish for privacy.

Then Ryan said something that made me smile despite all that
gloom. "Louie, we still get letters and emails asking about you and
how you're doing."

I was pleased to hear that viewers still remembered me and thought
enough about my work to write. I guess Huell's, "Louie, take a look at
this!" catchphrase had stuck. I thanked him for his kindness and shook

his hand again, bidding them all goodbye. Gloria and I walked away from the sad, emptying offices.

On the way to the car, I looked around the two former movie studios where I'd learned so much about television production and where I'd honed my craft. A feeling of deep loss swept over me. The two things that had been a big part of my career and life had come to an end: the shows Huell had created that I'd had the privilege of working on, and the KCET television lot. I looked forward to hearing from Ryan to help make some sense of all this, and hoped that, maybe over lunch, Huell and I could talk about all the questions that were left unanswered.

That lunch, however, didn't happen. Apparently Huell was quite ill and wasn't seeing people. Several months later, I did receive a call about him, but it wasn't from Ryan. It was from Ed Dahkaski, a good friend for over forty years since our days in college. I was happy to hear from him, as we hadn't talked for some time. I assumed he just wanted to catch up. But after we said our hellos, I instantly detected the concern in his voice. He asked why I hadn't attended KVCR's fiftieth-year broadcast celebration the week prior at the station's studio. Before I could answer his question with my own questions, beginning with, "What the hell celebration at KVCR are you talking about?" he said Huell had been there.

I shot back, "Huell was where? What are you talking about? I don't know anything about it!" This was the first I'd heard about the gathering to celebrate the station's golden anniversary. He said it had been a big happening, and he wondered why I didn't show. I told him no one from the station had tried to contact me. I felt hurt and disappointed and angry that I didn't have the chance to go and see Huell. (The station later apologized and said they'd emailed an invitation, which I'd never received—thanks, technology!)

Ed said, with hesitation in his voice, "He didn't look good, Luis, Huell didn't look good." He didn't know what was going on with Huell, but he could tell he wasn't well. And, of course, I hadn't been there to talk with Huell myself.

I thanked Ed for letting me know and hung up. I sat back in my chair and thought about Huell, wondering what was wrong, wondering what I could do. I called Ryan at the number he'd given me when we last saw each other and asked if I could see Huell. He was polite, but he was even firmer and more protective than the last time we talked. Huell was not seeing anyone, because he was too ill. I asked what was wrong with him, and Ryan merely replied that Huell was very sick, and he really couldn't say any more.

I was at an impasse. I couldn't find out about Huell's condition, and I knew I had to respect his wish for privacy. I asked Ryan to keep me posted and to let me know if they ever needed anything. He said, "Okay, Louie, we'll try to keep in touch."

I never heard back. Four months later, in early January of 2013, my friend Val Zavala, a spokesperson for KCET, called me to tell me that Huell had passed away. It turned out that he'd been battling prostate cancer for several years, but he was so private he just didn't want people to know.

The news was a blow, to say the least. It's strange how you can feel so shocked hearing that someone you care about has died, even if you knew they were very sick, but I know that's a universal experience. We are never prepared for someone to die.

Grief overcame me. I was sad that Huell had died, and I was also sad because I never got to see him, to talk to him about what was going on and see if I could be helpful. I wished I could have had the chance to raise his spirits with remembrances of our adventures together on the road shooting *California's Gold*.

Val asked if I would come out to the new KCET studios in Burbank that day. She was planning to do a special program about Huell, and she wanted me to share stories about him and the shows we did. Phil was there, too, and he and I told stories and talked about Huell as we knew him. I was happy to be there and pleased that Val had thought of me to appear on the program, but it was also unsettling. The program had a finality to it. It was a confirmation that Huell was truly gone.

After the special ended, I had the opportunity to meet with some of my old KCET friends who worked the cameras, sound, lights, and other technical work needed to produce a television program. They told me about the new studios, and we reminisced about the old times at the studio on Sunset Boulevard. Time sped by, as it always does when you're enjoying company and good conversation, and I realized it was getting late. I said my goodbyes, to some for the last time, and left.

The day had been long, and I was exhausted. Yet I will always cherish that day for giving me the opportunity to reveal, at long last, who "Louie" the cameraman was, and to share with his fans the happiness and sorrow I felt about the remarkable man named Huell Howser.

EPILOGUE

Well, that's the story of my adventures and time with Huell Howser on *California's Gold* and other television shows we did. I will always be grateful to Huell for the opportunity he gave me to be his cameraman, an experience that opened the door to the wonders of California and its people. Without him, I never would have had the chance to experience and enjoy all the things we discovered in the Golden State.

Now and then, I get letters addressed to me in care of *California's Gold*. Most of them are from viewers, sometimes viewers who are also professional photographers who want to tell me how much they have enjoyed my camera work, the way I shot particular episodes. I'm always grateful for those kind of letters, and to their writers who took the time to sit down and express their thoughts about the cameraman they have known only as the mysterious Louie.

If you'd like to learn more about Huell, *California's Gold*, and the other shows he did, I urge you to visit the Huell Howser Archives at the Leatherby Libraries located on the beautiful Chapman University campus in Orange, California. Huell left the body of his work to the university, including DVDs and tapes of many of his shows. As you enter the collection room, you'll discover a wall that takes you on a journey of his life from the time he was a little boy to his later years. Elsewhere, you'll encounter photos of Huell taken throughout his television career from Nashville to Los Angeles. Even pieces of his "found art" collection—objects he picked up during his travels in the desert—are on display. And his office is there too: his desk, chair, file cabinets, and schedule of shows on the wall, everything just as it was at KCET. You may reach into your imagination and see Huell sitting at his desk, dreaming up the next exciting California adventure to share with his audience.

Before you leave, don't forget to check the walls for the photo of Huell and me standing in front of the Golden Gate Bridge right after

Luis receiving Huell's honorary doctorate from Dr. James Doti, then president of Chapman University.

our shoot. It's on the cover of this book, and it's one of my favorites.

About a year after Huell's passing, I got a call from Ryan telling me that there was going to be an event at Chapman University to honor Huell with a doctorate degree. He asked if I'd be willing to go and accept the degree on his behalf. Of course, I said I'd be honored.

It was quite a night. There were about two thousand people in attendance: fans, friends, and colleagues who gathered to celebrate Huell's life and the imaginative and entertaining programs he had given them. They all loved him, and it was a beautiful thing to see.

When the time came to present the degree, I was introduced as *the* Louie, Huell's cameraman, and was asked to stand. I couldn't believe what happened next: The audience stood and applauded, giving rousing cheers for me. I was taken aback. All those years, I thought they knew me only vaguely as the unknown guy behind the camera. But I realized that they also knew me as Huell's shooting partner and friend.

As I held Huell's degree and witnessed the crowd's reaction, I was overcome with the thought of how much this doctorate would have meant to him. After a while, I handed it back, so they could put it in the archives with many of his personal effects.

I will never forget that day—how so many people came together to express an outpouring of love and gratitude for Huell Howser, who lives on in the hundreds of programs that continue to be treasured and aired on many television stations.

OUR
CALIFORNIA'S GOLD
SHOWS

This is not a complete guide to all the episodes—
just the ones we did together

1991

#201 Living History: Huell traveled to Fort Ross State Historical Park, where he experienced a nineteenth-century Russian community and he sailed aboard the *Californian*, the official "Tall Ship Ambassador" for the state of California.

#202 Central Coast: Huell visited San Luis Obispo and the surrounding area to see one of the state's oldest motels, Pozo's Saloon, Burgers, and Beers, and the Dunitas, the large sand dunes on the coast.

#203 LA to San Francisco Bay: Huell visited the famous South Central Los Angeles masterwork created by Italian immigrant Simon Rodia and then went to San Francisco to see how that city's famous sourdough bread is made.

#204 Head for the Borders: Huell enjoyed the Horseradish Festival in Tulelake near the Oregon border and drove down south to see the sights and sounds of Mexico in Calexico. He did his best to survive in a phone booth with a bunch of freshly ground horseradish.

#205 Santa Cruz: Huell went to Santa Cruz to visit the famous beach boardwalk and the last remaining oceanside amusement park in California. He rode the old wooden roller coaster that zooms down its first dip at fifty-five miles per hour. That shoot was a bit trying, but I had a lot of fun capturing Huell enjoying the ride.

#206 LA Adventures: To get a feel of the many aspects of Los Angeles, Huell visited the La Brea Tar Pits; Encounter Restaurant at LAX, Grand Central Market in downtown LA; the UCLA buried bridge; and Little Tokyo to see a 100-year-old grapefruit tree that still bears fruit. This show was pretty much all over the place, as Huell had not yet gotten into the familiar *California's Gold* style.

#207 Preserving the Past: Huell visited the town of Locke near Sacramento, founded and settled by the Chinese; traveled to Banning to hear ancient Cahuilla bird songs; then headed south to Vista to see antique farm vehicles and machinery in action. This show was actually the first *California's Gold* that Huell and I shot.

#208 Traditions: Huell went to a Mexican rodeo in Ontario; then up to Stockton to see the Stockton Ports minor league baseball team that is thought to have inspired the poem "Casey at the Bat,'" and from he was off to San Francisco to hear the Golden Gate Park Band.

#209 Trains: Huell celebrated train travel at Railfair '91 at the California State Railroad Museum in Sacramento and took a scenic train ride in the Mother Lode country. This was Huell's breakout show that set the standard for the rest of the *California's Gold* shows.

#210 Ships: Huell traveled to Trinidad Bay to meet an artisan who creates canoes from redwood logs; visited the SS *Polk*, a ship whose hull is made of concrete; and then he sailed on a lightship that is actually a floating lighthouse.

#211 Natural Wonders: Huell visited the tallest tree in Redwood National Park; walked among gorgeous fields of poppies, his favorite flower, in the Antelope Valley California Poppy Reserve near Lancaster; and climbed to the top of Morro Rock.

#212 Lost Sierra: Huell visited Downieville in the High Sierra for ski races; learned about the *Mountain Messenger*, the oldest Sierra newspaper; and checked out some heavy wooden skis worn by the gold miners.

1992

#301 Gold Country: Huell drove to the Sierra foothills to join in the Bidwell Bar Day celebration at Lake Oroville; visited the landmark Red Church (St. James Episcopal Church) in Sonora; and ended with a look at the Annual Poison Oak show in Columbia. He had a lot of fun with the idea of a poison oak festival.

#302 A Closer Look: Huell explored the sand dunes near El Centro to look at the remnants of the old plank road that was laid from Imperial County to Yuma, and then he attended a reunion of the Army's last mounted unit at Camp Lockett.

#303 Devil's Jaw: Huell traveled to Lompoc to investigate a 1923 naval disaster that occurred in dangerous waters off the coast, and then visited Mission La Purisma Concepción. (We did this segment on the mission before we shot the *California Missions* series.)

#304 Singing Cowboys: Huell drove up to Victorville to meet Roy Rogers and Dale Evans at their Victorville museum; then he met Herb Jeffries who starred in African American Westerns in the '30s; and he wound up the show by watching the Seventeenth Annual Black Cowboys Parade in Oakland.

#305 Blossom Trails: Huell traveled to Reedley in the Central Valley to see the fruit tree blossoms, but found only a few. So he ventured into "downtown" Reedley and found the Mennonite Quilt Center; sampled the Armenian delicacy called *keyma*, went to Uncle Harry's Classic Meals; and witnessed the world's longest-running pinochle game at the Camden Café. This show was a salvaged production, and Huell did an "amaaazing" job putting it together.

#306 Community Celebrations: Huell watched the Bok Kai Parade, California's oldest parade; celebrated the world's largest blossoming plant, a wistaria in Sierra Madre; and visited the Lincoln Memorial Shrine in Redlands.

#307 Buildings: Huell visited the old Carnegie Bayliss Branch Library in Glenn County; the Old Schoolhouse Museum in Twentynine Palms, the oldest building in Morongo Valley; and the Apple Pan in West Los Angeles, open since 1947.

#308 A Tale of Two Cities: Huell traveled to the Central Valley to visit Allensworth, a community founded by African Americans in the early 1900s; toured old and new Kernville; and finished up on the Kern River enjoying whitewater rafting. My strong swimming skills came in handy as I shot Huell just about every way I could in and out of the water.

#309 Things That Crawl in the Night: Huell explored the habitat of the kangaroo rat at the Carrizo Plain Natural Area in the Central Valley; then he went to the coast in San Pedro to experience a grunion run at Cabrillo Beach.

#310 Bodie: Huell made a thorough exploration of the old gold mining town that is the largest authentic ghost town in the Sierra Nevada.

#311 Mono Lake: Huell toured Mono Lake on the eastern side of the Sierra Nevada, and marveled at the tufa formations and scenic wonders of the beautiful body of water as he paddled its placid waters. Pretty pictures here.

#312 Nisei Parade and Little Tokyo: Huell discovered the history of the Japanese American community in downtown Los Angeles; celebrated

On the Mono Lake shoot, 1992.

the annual Nisei parade; and saw a traditional tea ceremony and beautiful bonsai and flower exhibits.

1993

#401 Buried Treasure: Huell explored the old town of Guadalupe off the Central Coast and searched for the lost set of Cecil B. DeMille's classic film *The Ten Commandments*, before traveling to the Sierra mining town of Allegheny in search of gold in a deep mine. Huell wore an Egyptian costume for the *Ten Commandments* part of the show.

Huell in costume for the "Buried Treasure" episode.

#402 Historic Horses: Huell visited the W.K. Kellogg Arabian Horse Center at Cal Poly Pomona and saw purebred Arabian horses put through their paces; then he journeyed to Sacramento to watch an exciting reenactment of the Pony Express, as it was during its two years in the Old West.

#403 Islands: Huell rode a bouncing ski boat from Long Beach to Catalina in an exciting and pounding ski race to the island and back; he then toured little-known San Nicolas Island in the Channel Islands. My shoulder was injured from the constant pounding on the rough water, and I had to undergo therapy after the shoot.

#404 Joshua Tree: Huell traveled to Joshua Tree National Park to see the world's tallest, oldest, and most interesting-looking Joshua trees; then he visited with a man who grew up on a ranch in what is now the national park. Huell loved the desert and doing shoots there. He had a home not far away.

#405 Our State's Front Yard: Huell visited the marvelously landscaped gardens and grounds of Capitol Park in Sacramento and discovered its beautiful flowers and plants, and he toured Memorial Grove, a grove of trees taken from the battlefields of the Civil War.

#406 Mariachi: Huell traced this old Mexican tradition from its beginnings in Jalisco, Mexico, to the present-day mariachi scene in Los Angeles; enjoyed the music of the world-famous Mariachi Los Camperos; and ended his musical journey with the student mariachi band at Garfield High School in East Los Angeles. I loved the way he said "mary-achi."

#407 Golden Gate Bridge: In one of his favorite *California's Gold* adventures, Huell saluted the striking bridge with a grand aerial tour around it, before going up into the structure to its windy top for a grand view of San Francisco and the Bay Area; he also talked with some of the original builders of the bridge and a painter who had the endless task

One of our many desert shoots.

of painting the bridge. This was my favorite *California's Gold* shoot and the most technically challenging—and rewarding.

#408 Angel Island: Huell toured the largest island in San Francisco Bay and explored its little-known history as a military installation and a detention center for Chinese immigrants from 1910 to '40.

#409 World War II: Huell explored a huge German-made crane at the Long Beach Naval Shipyard that was brought to America after the war, and he looked at the history of the 1942 shelling by a lone Japanese submarine of the Ellwood Oil Fields in Santa Barbara.

#410 Amboy: Huell traveled to the Mojave Desert in the heat of summer to explore the old Highway 66 town of Amboy; he also explored the huge Kelso Dunes and climbed the extinct Amboy Crater. I almost passed out in the heat climbing up Amboy Crater. It was 115 degrees with no shade. The things I did for Huell.

#411 Hard to Get to: Huell (and I) trekked a long distance up into the White Mountains to see bristlecone pines, the oldest living things on earth, and he visited beautiful LeConte Falls, set deep and remote in Yosemite Park. Huell loved nature, and being high up in bristlecone pine country was heaven for him.

#412 Terra Cotta: Huell toured the 118-year-old Gladding, McBean pottery company in Lincoln, near Sacramento, and discovered that it is the only remaining large manufacturer of architectural terra cotta in the United States. This is the one and only time that I fell while shooting a show.

1994

#501 Water under Pressure: Huell explored Malakoff Diggins State Park to see old hydraulic gold mining in the Sierra foothills; then got over to Calistoga to view the Old Faithful of California geyser, one of three in the world.

#502 Jack London: Huell visited Beauty Ranch, the former home of the famous author Jack London in the Valley of the Moon in Sonoma, which is now part of Jack London State Historic Park.

#503 California Companies: Huell toured two companies with roots in the Gold Rush: the Studebaker Car Company, which started out making wheelbarrows the miners used; and the original Levi Strauss & Company plant in San Francisco, where he saw one of the first pairs of jeans.

#504 Wings over California: Huell crossed the channel and took a flight with the Pigeon Courier Service at Avalon on Catalina Island; then he visited the Twentynine Palms Air Academy and took to the air in a glider. I got to fly, too.

#505 California's State Parks: Huell traveled to the Providence Mountains State Recreation Area in the Mojave Desert to see Mitchell Caverns Nature Preserve; then he visited Indian Grinding Rock State Historic Park to see ancient Miwok grinding pits.

#506 California Flowers: Huell visited Daffodil Hill in the Gold Country to see fields of the delicate flower; then he journeyed to the ranunculus fields at Carlsbad Ranch near the coast; and finished at the California Poppy Reserve in the Antelope Valley. I believe of the three flowers we shot, Huell loved the native poppies the most.

#507 San Luis Obispo Train: Huell enjoyed the centennial celebration of the railroad coming to town as the citizens re-created the events exactly as they occurred one hundred years ago, and then rode a period steam train into San Luis Obispo.

#508 Santa Barbara Island: Huell traveled to rugged Santa Barbara Island off California's coast to explore its history and experience the island with a ranger who lives there alone. There were narrow trails above sharp drops to the sea. Scary.

#509 Under California: Huell went to Fresno to see the incredible labyrinth of tunnels, rooms, and vines at the Underground Gardens of Baldassare Forestiere, then walked through the two thousand-foot Burro Schmidt Tunnel in the Mojave Desert, which took a miner fifty years to dig.

#510 Kelp: Huell went offshore into the Pacific from San Diego to Monterey to explore the great kelp forests off the California coast—he was shown how it grows, how it's harvested, and how it's used in many of the foods we eat.

#511 On Stage: Huell visited and heard the Spreckels Organ in Balboa Park, the world's largest outdoor organ, and went to Laguna Beach to see the Pageant of the Masters, the spectacular show of famous artworks brought to life by people posing exactly as in the artworks.

It was a treat to see the 're-creations.'

#512 Keeping Cool: Huell tried to keep cool in the hot Coachella Valley. He visited the old "desert submarine" of Indio and then went to Palm Springs to enjoy the cool of a lush oasis. This was one visit among many to the desert he loved, and where he lived later in his life.

1995

#601 Weed Patch: Huell visited a camp for migrant workers that had its start during the Dust Bowl era during the Depression, when the Okies fled to California and its promise of a better life. He talked to people who experienced life back then and to Latinos who live there now.

#602 Huts and Hangars: Huell toured the huge blimp hangar at the Marine Corps station at Tustin and got a little nervous in the two hundred-foot-high rafters; then he traveled to the Seabee Naval Museum at Port Hueneme to get a taste of the history of the naval builders; and ended the trip with a visit to the Marine Corps Base Camp at Pendleton to check out an old quonset hut.

#603 Olives and Berries: Huell explored the olive orchards of the San Joaquin Valley and then visited the old Graber Olive Company in Ontario to see the processing methods; next he went to Knott's Berry Farm to learn how the amusement park grew from a simple beginning of great home cooking. I still visit Graber's every year to say hello and to buy their tasty olives.

#604 Important Places: Huell traveled to Camp Pendleton, north of San Diego, to see a camp where, in the 1970s, thousands of Vietnamese refugees lived in a tent city; then he visited the Sherman Indian High School in Riverside and see a school that has educated Native Americans for almost a century.

#605 Hidden Gold: Huell dug deep and visited the La Brea Tar Pits to see the creatures that died there and have been preserved in the oily goo for thousands of years; then he went to the Presidio of San Diego to see the excavation of the first European settlement in California.

#606 Life in Death Valley: Huell discovered the living wonders of Death Valley, such as the prehistoric pup fish that have survived for thousands of years; and he walked among the wildflowers that thrive in the valley, despite its harsh climate.

#607 Scotty's Castle: Huell returned to Death Valley, this time to tour the castle and look into the life of Walter Scott, the colorful man for whom the famous castle was named.

#608 Center of California: Huell searched for the geographic center of California, traveling to various locations where local groups claimed that their spot is the true center of the state. He found the real one. Huell also visited an area on old Highway 99 that is planted with palms and pines, marking the divide between Northern and Southern California.

#609 Oil: Huell visited the vast Midway-Sunset Oil Field in Kern County, the largest producing field in the lower forty-eight states; he saw an old wooden derrick, the last of its kind; and he learned about the Lakeview gusher that once spewed millions of gallons of oil for eighteen straight months.

#610 California Zephyr: Huell traveled on the train that ran from Chicago to Oakland from 1949 to '70; Huell loved trains, so on the long trip he had fun visiting with and talking to oldtimers who worked on and traveled on the original Zephyr.

#611 Folsom Prison: Huell toured Folsom State Prison, which houses some of the state's toughest prisoners; he saw Folsom's first death row and visited the seldom-seen graveyard where generations of prisoners were laid to rest. I don't think I have ever been as anxious on a *California's Gold* shoot as I was on this one.

#612 McCloud: Huell visited the historic lumber and railroad town at the foot of Mt. Shasta; rode the rails through a forest on the famous McCloud Railway; then visited the local swimming hole before touring the old town. This area was one of Huell's favorites to visit, and it seems we were there often.

1996

#701 Lighthouse: Huell took a helicopter trip to visit the century-old abandoned St. George Reef Lighthouse located eight miles off the coast of Crescent City; he toured the old relic and marveled that it has withstood the most violent seas. This was one of my favorite shoots, and I shot it as if it were a film.

#702 California Pools: Huell profiled famous swimming pools, beginning at the Hollywood Roosevelt Hotel, then the LA Memorial Coliseum swimming pool built for the 1932 Olympics, then to the Neptune Pool at Hearst Castle. This "wet" tour ended at two pools in San Francisco that are now gone: the Fleishacker Pool and Sutro Baths.

#703 California Firsts: Huell learned the story of the "real" first discovery of gold in California, in Placerita Canyon; then he looked at the spot of the first oil drilling; and he finished with the discovery of a location where an innovation in the history of electricity took place.

#704 Mare Island: Huell toured the historic Mare Island Naval Shipyard, which had served the nation for 142 years but was slated to be closed; he visited with people who helped build battleships up to nuclear subs through the years; and finally he visited a sailor's graveyard and the first naval chapel on the West Coast.

Huell in his beloved Yosemite.

#705 Suisun Bay: Huell toured the great mothballed fleet of hundreds of navy ships at Suisun Bay. He marveled at the assortment of ships that are kept there in reserve—everything from tankers to cruisers, many of them historic.

#706 Yosemite Fire Fall: Huell journeyed to the top of Glacier Point to see the spot from which red-hot coals were once pushed off the side to create a glowing "waterfall" rushing downto the valley below. Huell visited with the couple who ran the nightly show for forty-two years until it ended in 1969.

#707 Neat Houses: Huell traveled to Sacramento to visit the former Governor's Mansion, which was used from 1903 to '67. Kathleen Brown took Huell on a tour of the house; and then he headed east to the Sierra foothills to visit a sharply contrasting rustic log cabin built by miners.

#708 Dry Lake Bed: Huell visited the old Muroc Dry Lake bed, now the home of Edwards Air Force Base, to see a gathering of race cars and the oldtimers who once raced on the lake bed before the Air Force made it off-limits.

#709 Camels and Bison: Huell traveled to Catalina Island to see a herd of bison that started out fourteen strong, brought over to be used in a silent movie; then trekked to Fort Tejon State Historic Park to see where camels were introduced by the Army in the 1850s to see if they could be used as effective transportation. It turns out they couldn't.

#710 San Juan Bautista: Huell visited the historic town of San Juan Bautista, which was for many years a center of commerce and meetings of people from all walks of life. He also visited the town's mission, which was founded in 1787 and is still used as a parish church.

#711 Santa Rosa Island: Huell explored Santa Rosa Island, one of the Channel Islands, and investigated its rich history from the time of the Chumash through a visit by Cabrillo to its current use as a working cattle ranch run by two brothers. Huell accompanied a real cattle drive to a waiting boat.

#712 Japanese Tea Garden: Huell traveled to Golden Gate Park in San Francisco to walk through its authentic Japanese Tea Garden, which has been a lovely setting for more than one hundred years. Huell enjoyed the flowering cherry trees and new discoveries along its paths and bridges. He jumped from one thing to another without telling me, and following him around, tested me. The show, however, came out fine.

1997

#801 Quicksilver: Huell visited the New Almaden Mine, the first mining community in California, established in 1845. Located in the Santa Clara Valley near San Jose, the mercury mine proved to the richest mine of any kind ever in California.

#802 Railcars: Huell traveled to the annual US National Handcar Race at the California State Railroad Museum in Sacramento and watched the contestants pump away to the finish. Then he traveled to McCloud Railway to ride along in motorized "speeders" that are used to inspect the railroad tracks. Did we do trains!

#803 Rocks in Water: Huell went out on Lake Tahoe and climbed Emerald Rock, the only island on the lake; then he went to Humboldt Bay to see the massive concrete interlocking shapes that protect the bay from harsh seas; finally, he traveled to the Mojave Desert and discovered strange assortments of rocks, far from the water today but they were actually fish traps made by Native Americans when long ago there was lake water there.

#804 Mt. San Jacinto: Huell took us up the steep rise of the Palm Springs Aerial Tramway, which climbs from the desert floor to Mt. San Jacinto, more than ten thousand feet high; then back to the base of the mountain to explore the thirteen-mile tunnel that was dug during the 1930s to bring Colorado River water to Southern California.

#805 Wooden Boats: Huell returned to Lake Tahoe to attend the Annual Concours d' Elegance, which celebrates the beautiful wooden boats that have plied the waters of the lake since the 1920s. He enjoyed a ride on one of these speedsters on the beautiful waters of the Sierra lake.

#806 Slab City: Huell went to the Coachella Valley to see Salvation Mountain, artist Leonard Knight's colorful monument of sculpture, trees, flowers, and the American flag built into a mountainside; then he went down the road to visit Slab City, a community of some three thousand people, many of them colorful characters, who live rent free and very independently on an abandoned Marine base.

#807 Paradise: Huell explored the town of Paradise in Butte County for the annual Gold Nugget Days Celebration, which commemorates the discovery of a fifty-four-pound gold nugget that was pulled out of the earth in nearby Dogtown; visited the spot where the huge nugget was found; and then toured the Gold Nugget Museum, which houses memorabilia from the gold mining period.

#808 Mule Days: Huell joined the Mule Days Celebration in Bishop, on the east side of the Sierra Nevada. The weeklong fête recognizes the role mules played in the old mining days, when they hauled materials and ore for the miners.

#809 Wind: Huell went to the Warner Brothers lot in Burbank to see a movie wind machine in action; then he went to Caltech in Pasadena to see the ten-foot wind tunnel that's been used to test everything from cars to airplanes; finally, he journeyed to Point Reyes, to feel the *real* wind at the windiest place in California.

#810 Bits and Pieces: All of the segments in this show came about from chance discoveries along our travels. Huell visited an ostrich farm in Buellton; he had a lot of fun stumbling onto a flowering field of marigolds not far from Ventura; he toured a historic two-story out-house in San Juan Batista; and he explored a cactus farm operation in the Salinas Valley.

#811 Vandenberg: Huell visited Vandenberg Air Force Base on the coast near the town of Lompoc. As he toured the rocket launching site, he discovered that the base has played an important part in the devel-opment and use of rockets and boosters for both military programs and civilian satellite launches.

#812 Snow and Ice: Huell went to the Sierra Nevada in winter to inves-tigate the history of ice harvesting from frozen mountain lakes—the source of ice before refrigeration; then he traveled from Sacramento to Reno to see the last of the snow-shed tunnels that were built to shield the rails from the great mountain snows. I remember this as the coldest shoot we did. Brrrrrr.

1998

#901 San Miguel Island: Huell traveled to San Miguel Island with a group that re-created the landing in 1542 of the Spanish explorer Juan Rodriguez Cabrillo; he also had a pleasant and insightful visit with a woman who lived on the island with her parents in the 1930s and '40s.

#902 Coloma: Huell visited Marshall Gold Discovery State Historic Park to see the place where, in 1848, James Marshall picked up the gold nugget that started the California Gold Rush. He visited with a living-history group that celebrates the times of the miners, wearing exact replicas of the clothing of the era.

#903 Blue Angels: Huell traveled to El Centro to visit with the famous Blue Angels Navy Aerobatic Team, which has been thrilling spectators for almost seventy years. He accepted the invitation of a lifetime to fly in an F/A-18 Hornet jet and experienced the team's flying maneuvers. After he got back on solid ground, he promptly threw up. Good timing, I'd say.

#904 Guadalupe: Huell explored the picturesque and quaint town of Guadalupe, not far from the coast. He toured the town, admiring its old-time look, talked with townspeople who'd been there for generations, and went out into lettuce and celery fields to experience the harvest. Finally, Huell visited the spectacular, windswept Guadalupe-Nipomo Dunes.

#905 Delta Queen: Huell traveled 1,500 miles to the Mississippi River to ride on the *Delta Queen*, a boat that plies the river in grand style. Its connection to California is that it was built in the 1920s and sailed the Sacramento River until 1947, when it was shipped east via the Panama Canal to ride on the Big River.

#906 China Clipper: Huell went to San Francisco's Treasure Island to visit the home of the old China Clippers, luxurious "flying boats" that flew from the City by the Bay to the Far East beginning in the mid-1930s, but lasting for only five years.

#907 San Luis Obispo Chinatown: Huell visited the historic Chinese community in San Luis Obispo that was settled by immigrants who built the railroads and worked in the fields. Huell was treated to a lion dance put on by Chinese students at the nearby university.

#908 See's Candies: Huell traveled to San Francisco to visit one of the earliest See's stores. He talked with customers about the candies they liked and asked why they were loyal to See's Candies, and he sampled a few. Then he returned to Los Angeles to tour the factory that makes all those delicious varieties. He ate candy throughout the shoot, and was as happy as I'd ever seen him.

With the big trucks.

#909 Big Things in the Desert: Huell went to the desert near Palm Springs to see the giant windmills at one of the largest wind farms in the world; then he traveled farther into the desert to see the US Borox Boron Mine near the town of Boron and to show you the immense trucks that haul the boron out of a large hole in the desert; finally, he trekked to Goldstone in a remote part of the Mojave, where he inspected and climbed atop one of the Deep Space Network's huge antennas. The little boy in Huell had the time of his life on those shoots.

#910 Citrus Gold: Huell talked with a collector who's an expert on the thousands of colorful labels that were once affixed to orange crates. Then he traveled to UC Riverside to view and walk through the orchards where the university conducts research on the thousands of citrus trees it grows.

#911 Arrowhead Springs: Huell trekked to the famous natural "arrowhead" landmark on the side of a mountain in the San Bernardino Mountains. Then he visited the old Arrowhead Springs Hotel, which was a playground for Hollywood stars in the 1940s and '50s; finally, he toured the many hot mineral springs that drew the stars and continue to spew hot water.

#912 Shasta Dam: Huell explored Shasta Dam, which holds back Shasta Lake. He marveled at the size of the structure and how it was built over a period of seven years starting in 1938. He talked with old-timers who were involved in the construction of the huge dam, whose spillway is three times higher than that of Niagara Falls. The dam was impressive.

1999

#1001 Salt: Huell traveled to the salt ponds near San Francisco to see how salt is made through the evaporation process. He toured Cargill's facility, which makes 300,000 tons of salt a year from the ponds.

#1002 Hidden Alcatraz: Huell toured the famous island and its infamous prison, which housed the most dangerous of the state's convicts. He discovered its earlier history as a prison for Southern privateers during the Civil War and learned that the old structures were covered when the newer prison was built atop them. He also toured the dark and musty catacombs beneath the prison.

#1003 Kaiser Shipyard: Huell discovered the important role that the Kaiser Shipyard played during WWII: building hundreds of ships. He talked with people who worked in the shipyard then, including some "Rosie the Riveters" women. He visited the SS *Red Oak Victory*, which was built there and preserved by the city of Richmond.

#1004 San Onofre Beach: Huell visited San Onofre, whose legendary waves attract surfers from near and far. He talked with older surfers from the San Onofre Surfing Club who have honed their skills off that beach for decades, and he spoke with surfers who ride longboards.

#1005 Things That Come Back: Huell visited the site of the ancient Tulare Lake, once the largest freshwater lake west of the Great Salt Lake. Farmers dried it up in the 1930s, but now and then during wet winters it comes back in a smaller form. Huell enjoyed a canoe ride in the now-and-then mini-lake. He also went to the site of Sutter's Mill to check out the story of a woman named Jenny Wimmer, the person who took the nugget that James Marshall found and tested it to prove that it was indeed gold.

#1006 Trestle: Huell traveled downstate to the San Diego area to ride a railcar that took him and a group of ex-railroad employees on old tracks that ran from San Diego to Arizona. He explored the old curved wooden Goat Canyon Trestle, a wonder of engineering, and ended the ride at a blocked tunnel.

#1007 Muscle Beach: Huell visited the famous oceanfront site just south of the Santa Monica Pier, where from 1934 to 1959 fitness buffs and musclemen tumbled and built human pyramids and posed for gawkers. He also interviewed seniors who back in the day were the daring performers of Muscle Beach.

#1008 Wine: Huell visited one of the oldest wineries in California, which had its beginnings in 1904 in the Rancho Cucamonga area of Southern California. He was amazed to learn that the Guasti Winery once owned four thousand acres of wine grapes, making it the largest winery in the world. Huell also attended a reunion of old workers who told him stories of what life was like when they lived and worked there.

#1009 Flying Fish: Huell took a seagoing trip on the *Flying Fish Boat,* which was built especially by William Wrigley Jr. to view the flying fish at night around Catalina Island. Two powerful spotlights illuminated the water, and the fish came up and flew over the bow. Huell also traveled back to Catalina to interview Wrigley's granddaughter, who shared some wonderful stories.

#1010 Lompoc Mural: Huell ventured to Lompoc to visit the site of a twelve-acre American flag made of flowers that were planted at the beginning of World War II as a salute to the Americans fighting in the war. Huell discovered that the last planting was in 1952. He visited a mural of the American flag that was painted by local artists as a celebration of the original flower flag.

#1011 Devil's Postpile: Huell trekked through rugged country in the Sierra to visit the famous volcanic site that 100,000 years ago was molten rock. He marveled at the sixty-foot-high pile of stone that split into columns as it cooled, forming its odd, geometric shape. I took enough equipment to shoot a movie.

#1012 Abalone: Huell investigated the history of abalone at Point Lobos State Reserve, learning that it goes back to the Native Americans, who ate them and used the shells as decoration and for trade. He also visited the site where Japanese abalone fishermen first harvested them commercially. And, he cooked up some abalone with school kids.

2000

#2001 First Theater: Huell traveled to Monterey to explore early theatrical productions in California that got going in 1847 in a makeshift theater that was really a saloon and boardinghouse. He got to see a performance in the original theater. He then went up the state to Sacramento to the Eagle Theater, which was built in 1849 to entertain the hordes of gold miners who had come to seek their fortune.

#2002 Point Sur Lighthouse: Huell explored the history of the lighthouse that from the late 1800s has been guiding ships safely away from the treacherous rocks. He then toured the National Historic Landmark's buildings, where families once lived with the operators of the old lighthouse.

#2003 Swallows: Huell traveled downstate to Mission San Juan Capistrano, where, on March 19th, Saint Joseph's Day, swallows that have traveled for thousands of miles return to nest in the safety of the old mission. (Sadly, very few return these days.) Huell enjoyed the festivities that surround the "miracle" return of the swallows.

#2004 Bird Rock: Huell went across the water near Catalina Island to explore a tiny island that is privately owned by a family. He explored the island with the owners and marveled at the numbers of birds that have made the little island their home. That was a messy shoot, as the birds use the rock as their bathroom.

#2005 Mud Pots: Huell journeyed to the southern end of the Coachella Valley to the Imperial Wildlife Area to explore the bubbling mud pots that gurgle and pop constantly. Then he went to visit another area on private land and enjoyed some more extraordinary mud pots. He enjoyed playing in the mud.

#2006 Hot Creek: Huell traveled to the east side of the Sierra to a creek not far from Mammoth. He delighted in his discovery that what made the water unique was the hot water bubbling up and mixing with the cold, snowmelt creek water to make for a comfortable swimming experience.

#2007 Nixon's Birthplace: Huell made the short trip to Yorba Linda to the President's childhood home and site of the Richard Nixon Library. Julie Nixon Eisenhower gave Huell a personal tour of the home and delighted him with stories of her father's boyhood there.

#2008 San Francisco Cemeteries: Huell traveled to San Francisco to get the story of what happened to the cemeteries in San Francisco. He learned that as the city grew, demand for land also grew, and bodies that had been interred were dug and up reburied elsewhere, their headstones used to build breakwaters and for paving. He visited two remaining old cemeteries, including the grounds at Mission San Francisco de Asís, and he visited the San Francisco Columbarium.

#2009 Historic Chickens: Huell traveled upstate to Petaluma to attend the annual Butter and Egg Days celebration commemorating the city's once-held honor of being the "largest poultry center in the world." In 1916, Petaluma shipped more than eleven million dozen eggs. Huell then toured decaying original chicken houses and talked with people who'd grown up on the chicken ranches.

#2010 State Library Treasures: Huell traveled to Sacramento to discover the historical riches housed in the California State Library. He viewed a seventeenth-century map of California and James Marshall's own hand-drawn map and sketch of his gold discovery. Huell loved this piece of California history.

#2011 Under Lake Arrowhead: Huell traveled up into the San Bernardino Mountains to Lake Arrowhead. Instead of marveling at the beautiful lake, Huell went down a 100-foot shaft to explore the tunnels under the lake that were once slated to be used as part of an irrigation project that didn't come to pass.

#2012 Monarchs: Huell traveled to Pismo State Beach to see the hundreds of thousands of monarch butterflies that journey from Mexico to winter at this site; it's the world's largest concentration of the delicate flying creatures.

#2013 Emperor and the President: Huell journeyed to San Francisco, Sonoma, and Red Bluff to investigate the colorful history of two men. The first, by proclamation of his fellow citizens after the Bear Flag Revolt of 1846, was dubbed the president of California. The other was a gentleman, who, in the 1800s, proclaimed himself to be "Emperor of the United States and Protector of Mexico."

2001

#3001 Clear Lake: Huell traveled to Clear Lake at the base of Mt. Konocti to explore California's largest natural lake. He discovered the rich Native American history that was evident at the lake as he explored its marshes and waters. He also toured wonderful oak groves that are as pristine today as they were in prehistoric times.

#3002 Dune Buggy: Huell went to the San Bernardino Mountains to see a dune buggy show that featured Bruce Meyers's dune buggy creations, which set records for overland travel on rough and remote roads. He took a wild ride in a dune buggy that had him shouting "Whoa, whoa!" to the driver, who was shooting up steep banks and really going fast on the rough roads.

#3006 Zamboni: Huell traveled to the Arrowhead Pond of Anaheim, home of the Mighty Ducks hockey team, to see the ice-grooming machine called a Zamboni smooth the ice. He learned about its inventor, whose name is like Kleenex and Windex when it comes to machines that groom ice. He toured the Zamboni factory with the son of the inventor and saw how these machines were made.

#3007 Will Rogers: Huell drove up into the hills above Sunset Boulevard near the Pacific Ocean to Will Rogers State Historic Park to explore the summer home of the beloved philosopher, actor, and commentator who lived there from 1928 to '44. He got a personal tour of the home from Will's last remaining child, Jimmie Rogers, who regaled Huell with stories about the house and of his memories growing up there.

#3009 Glass Beaches: Huell explored two beaches that are treasure-hunter's paradises. He went to Fort Bragg on the northern coast to visit Glass Beach, where a dump was once located. The pounding waves over time polished the dump's broken bottles and created "gems" that people collect. Then he went to Patrick's Point State Park north of Eureka. There, at Agate Beach, Huell discovered more natural gems polished by wave action. This is the last *California's Gold* that I shot for Huell.

Louie toasting Huell after accepting his honorary doctorate at Chapman University.

ACKNOWLEDGMENTS

We wish to thank Dr. Sheryl Bourgeois, executive vice-president of university advancement at Chapman University, for providing us open access to the works that Huell donated to the university, and for allowing us to use photos and material for the book. We are grateful. We'd also like to thank Rand Boyd, special collections and archives librarian at the Leatherby Libraries, for his help with our efforts to examine the files, tapes, photos, and memorabilia in the Huell Howser Collection at Chapman University. There was a *lot* of material to sift through, because Huell kept just about everything that had to do with his education and television careers. The files even included newspaper clippings of his activities in high school. Lauren Menges and John Encarnacion were also incredibly helpful over at the archives, and deserve many thanks for their hard work and patience.

We want to thank the many people interviewed for this book for their informative, personal, and heartwarming stories, which revealed what Huell meant to them beyond his role as a television personality. And we'd like to thank the people at KCET for their generous assistance in securing photos for the book.

We especially want to thank Angel Diaz, the former *California's Gold* archivist at the Leatherby Libraries, who lived up to her name, for cheerfully helping us make our way through the considerable collection of material covering Huell's life and career that he left to the library. Her organization was confounding at times, but that's because she used logic and a bit of creativity to organize and file Huell's archives—but, of course, everything was exactly where it should have been, and we are deeply indebted to her.

Finally, we're grateful to the people at Prospect Park Books, especially publisher Colleen Dunn Bates, who made the book possible; designer Amy Inouye; assistant editor Dorie Bailey, and the rest of the editorial team: Margery Schwartz, Emily Peters, and Elizabeth Ovieda.

INDEX

ABOUT THE AUTHORS

LUIS FUERTE is the five-time Emmy-award-winning former camera-man for the Huell Howser show *California's Gold*, a hugely popular program that continues to run on California's many PBS stations even since Howser's death in 2013. The son of a Mexican immigrant, Fuerte was born in San Bernardino, California. He became a cameraman after two years in the US Navy and attending LA Valley College to study television engineering. Besides his Emmy awards, Fuerte has been named Latino of the Year, been inducted into two halls of fame, and won the Golden Mic Award, the International Monitor Award, and the Salt of the Earth Award. After forty-eight years in television, he's now retired and lives with his wife in Rialto, California.

DAVID DURON met Luis Fuerte while working as senior unit man-ager at KCET-TV in Los Angeles. A Marine Corps veteran who earned bachelor's in political science and a master's degree in journalism from UCLA, he also wrote and produced for KCBS-TV and KABC-TV during his television career. Now retired from a real job, Duron is working on several writing projects, including a novel and other as-told-to books from his home in Yucaipa, California.